# THE ART OF INVESTIGATIVE PSYCHODYNAMIC THERAPY

# THE ART OF
# INVESTIGATIVE PSYCHODYNAMIC
# THERAPY

## THE GERWE ORCHESTRATION METHOD (G-OM)

Corinne F. Gerwe

Algora Publishing
New York

Library of Congress Cataloging-in-Publication Data —

Gerwe, Corinne F.
    The art of investigative psychodynamic therapy: the Gerwe Orchestration Method
(G-OM) / developed by Corinne F. Gerwe.
        p. cm.
    Includes bibliographical references.
    ISBN 978-0-87586-654-3 (trade pbk.: alk. paper) 1. Psychodynamic psychotherapy.
2. Post-traumatic stress disorder. I. Title.
    RC489.P72G47 2010
    616.89'14—dc22
                                        2010008222

Printed in the United States

# TABLE OF CONTENTS

INTRODUCTION: THE GERWE ORCHESTRATION METHOD (G-OM) OVERVIEW       1
    *Co-Occurring Substance Use Disorders (SUDs) and PTSD Treatment*       1
    *Step 1: Assessment Questionnaire*       2
    *Step 2: Introduction to the Orchestration Group Process (OGP) Rules and Guidelines*       2
        *The OGP "Conductor"*       3
    *Step 3: Introduction to the OGP Tools and Worksheets*       4
        *The G-OM Lifespan Chart*       4
        *The Level of Intensity Meter*       5
        *The Daily Prediction Scale (DPS)*       5
    *Step 4: Monitoring the Symptoms: Physical Memory = Rapid Response*       8
    *Step 5: Treating the Behavior with Alternative Behavioral Strategy Planning*       9
    *Step 6: Composing Strategies and Creating Solutions*       9
    *Step 7: Conducting a Plan and Evaluating Risk*       9
    *Step 8: A Step-by-Step guide that demonstrates compatibility between G-OM and*
        *the 12-Step Program*       10
    *Step 9: The Finale: G-OM Exit Questionnaire*       10
    *Supportive Research*       10
    *Conclusion*       10

CHAPTER 1. INVESTIGATING THE PHENOMENON OF PIVOTAL EXPERIENCE       13
    *Step 1: G-OM Assessment of Behavioral Health (ABH)*       13
    *Novel Experience*       14
    *Why Investigate And Identify Pivotal Experiences From The Past?*       15
    *Case Example*       16
    *Breaking Down Pivotal Experience into Identifiable Components*       17
    *THE G-OM ASSESSMENT QUESTIONNAIRE FOR BEHAVIORAL HEALTH (ABH)*       23
    *G-OM-ABH TEMPLATE SUMMARY*       26
    *G-OM-ABH Template Summarized Example #1*       28
    *G-OM-ABH Template Summarized Example #2*       29
    *Advantages of the ABH*       29

CHAPTER 2. EXPLORING THE ORIGIN AND PATH OF THE CORE PROBLEM       31
    *Step 2: The Orchestration Group Process (OGP)*       31

OGP Implementation | 35
Core Components of the Orchestration Group Process Method | 35
The OGP "Conductor" | 36
The Orchestration Group Process in Session | 40
Orchestration Group Documentation | 49

CHAPTER 3. CHARTING THE LIFESPAN FROM PAST TO PRESENT | 55
Step 3: The OGP Tools and Worksheets | 55
Vivid Core Memory | 56
Illustrated Memory Impression | 57
Memory | 57
Key Tools Surrounding OGP | 59
Origin and Evolution of the Level of Intensity Meter | 62
The Daily Prediction Scale | 62
Daily Prediction Scale (DPS) | 63
Memory Episode Dynamic (MED) | 66
Prioritizing Identified Pivotal Experiences | 67
Memory Episode Dynamic Worksheet | 67

CHAPTER 4. MONITORING THE SYMPTOMS THAT UNDERLIE AND EMERGE | 69
Step 4: "Physical Memory = Rapid Response" PTSD Symptom Identification and
Treatment | 69
The "Orchestration" of the Human Body | 69
Physical Symptom Evolution and Longevity | 72
Physical Memory = Rapid Response | 73
G-OM Examples of Identified Feeling Responses | 74
G-OM Examples of Identified Physical Symptoms | 76
Conclusions | 83

CHAPTER 5. TREATING THE BEHAVIOR TO DIMINISH ITS POWER | 85
Step 5: G-OM Alternative Behavioral Planning | 85
Case Example of Pattern Evolution, Skill, Ability and Innovation | 91
Alternative Behavior Worksheet | 97
Summary | 97
Feeling and Behavior Combination | 97

CHAPTER 6. COMPOSING STRATEGIES & CREATING SOLUTIONS | 101
Step 6: Workshops, G-OM Group Compositions, and Individual Session Questionnaire | 101
G-OM 5-Question Group Composition | 102
GROUP RECORDER (MED) WORKSHEET | 104
G-OM Small Group Compositions | 106
G-OM INDIVIDUAL SESSION QUESTIONNAIRE #1 | 107
G-OM INDIVIDUAL SESSION QUESTIONNAIRE #2 | 108

CHAPTER 7. CONDUCTING A PLAN AND EVALUATING RISK | 111
Step 7: The Aftercare Planning Session: Risk Evaluation and Assessment | 111
G-Om Aftercare Planning Checklist | 111
High Risk Identification & Evaluation: The Potential Toward Relapse Scale (PTRS) | 114
Chronic Relapse Screening Instrument | 115
A High-Risk Case Example: Ryan: A Risk Not Identified | 116

CHAPTER 8. ARRANGING COLLABORATIONS FOR SUPPORT AND SUCCESS | 123
Step 8: Behavioral Development and the 12-Step Program | 123
The Twelve Steps of Alcoholics Anonymous | 125

CHAPTER 9. THE FINALE: THE G-OM EXIT QUESTIONNAIRE | 133

# INTRODUCTION: THE GERWE ORCHESTRATION METHOD (G-OM) OVERVIEW

## CO-OCCURRING SUBSTANCE USE DISORDERS (SUDS) AND PTSD TREATMENT

"Come, Watson, come!" he cried. "The game is afoot. Not a word! Into your clothes and come!" —Sir Arthur Conan Doyle, "The Adventures of the Abbey Grange," *The Return of Sherlock Holmes*

The Gerwe Orchestration Method (G-OM) was developed to identify and address persistent emotional/behavioral conditions stemming from pivotal/traumatic life-altering experiences. Case study research conducted during the early stages of G-OM development indicated a high correlation between high impact developmental experiences and a propensity toward substance abuse upon first initiation and subsequent substance abuse disorders (SUDs) and SUDs chronicity (Gerwe, 2000, 2007). Continued development of G-OM recognized similar compounding conditions from later high-impact life-experiences that had consistent PTSD symptom factors identified more in relation to the pivotal experiences than SUDs onset and progression. SUDs appeared to be a co-occurring disorder post or coinciding with conditions stemming from extreme/novel life events.

Treatment for these conditions using G-OM investigates the experiential history of each person in order to identify crucial lifespan episodes and the nature of their impact on the individual. A psychodynamic group process, the Gerwe Orchestration Group Process (OGP) was created for this purpose. OGP helps the collective group understand the consistent dynamics that can occur during and after extreme/traumatic experiences. OGP experientially demonstrates how these consistencies, when ineffectively addressed and/or not resolved can develop into repetitive continually evolving emotional conditions and respondent behavioral patterns that, over time, can become deeply entrenched in the personality of the individual and the neuronal structure of the brain.

G-OM can be implemented at the initial stage of treatment within a case-management or other clinical structure. The ideal situation would involve an 8-week program with four three-hour sessions of G-OM per week built within the case-management activities. G-OM is manualized and has many assessment and worksheet tools, and small work-group exercises that support the Orchestration Group Process (OGP). The following overview outlines the G-OM order of procedure. The following chapters describe the G-OM in detail with illustrations.

STEP 1: ASSESSMENT QUESTIONNAIRE

The program begins with the Gerwe Assessment for Behavioral Health (ABH). ABH is the first G-OM exercise in identifying the most predominant current feeling states, associated physical symptoms, and related behavioral responses of the individual, their approximate period of origin, and the approximate percentage of time these symptoms are generated within each current 24-hour period.

Note: The ABH has been unofficially implemented within military clinical treatment and is believed by many to have enormous potential in benefiting the military and returning soldiers struggling with internal controls, violence, post-traumatic stress, substance abuse, and the isolation experienced when unable to relate to loved ones back home. ABH was implemented for three years within a criminal justice system pilot project studying the G-OM within the over-all study of their project resulting is favorable outcomes and ongoing implementation.

STEP 2: INTRODUCTION TO THE ORCHESTRATION GROUP PROCESS (OGP) RULES AND GUIDELINES

This involves a 20 minute overview of instruction and group configuration demonstration. The structure of the group creates boundaries that represent the identifiable components of life-altering experiences revealed in hundreds of documented cases upon which G-OM was founded. This structured approach, addressing what for many erupts as persistent overwhelming emotional/physical distress conditions, dependent on behavior that was constructed to relieve them, helps the individual begin to understand the driving factors associated with their most problematic emotional states and actions. Thus, increased insight and ability to identify their own individual reaction formation to extreme events forms the basis for creating therapeutic and cognitive/behavioral treatment strategies directly related to these formations, rather than a generalized approach.

When the introduction is completed, the group process can immediately follow. OGP is both educational and experiential as each participant begins to reveal individual reactions to experiences shared by one person per session. OGP engages each person into an active and collaborative role in a process that generates self-understanding and insight, motivation, and a reframed self-concept that supports personal growth actions and meaningful recovery.

### The OGP "Conductor"

OGP is led by the facilitator/conductor. The conductor is responsible for the pace and flow of the process. The conductor is the guiding force, the behavioral example, and is responsible for exemplifying objectivity, compassion and investigative courage while ensuring the structure and integrity of the process. The Conductor prepares the room prior to the group therapy session by drawing the Memory Episode Dynamic on a blackboard. It is also a visual representation of how the group is structured and serves as a backdrop to the group conductor and soloist and should be in direct vision of the group participants. Only one experience is shared per group process. The conductor will write the identified information as it is disclosed by the soloist in the appropriate circular sections of the visual concept.

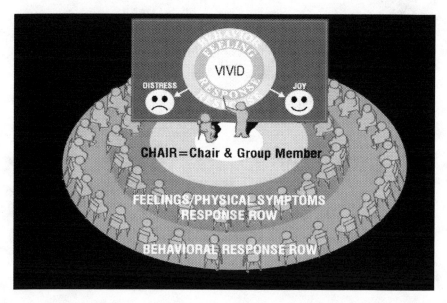

**The Soloist:** The group member chosen as soloist should be well acquainted with the OGP and should have participated in the group process prior to being chosen as a volunteer. The conductor can then better assess level of stabilization and who is most appropriate for this role. The soloist should be chosen based on his or her desire to share an experience that is regularly present in thoughts as memory. In OGP, it is never appropriate to probe for memories that the person does not have, or pressure someone to volunteer. It is not necessary for every member of group to be a soloist.

**The Feelings and Behavior Rows:** The feeling row is the ideal place for a new participant to begin once a regular group has been established. Feeling row participants are instructed to try to imagine what they might have felt if the experience shared by the soloist had happened to them. They will also be asked to describe physical symptoms that typically occur when the feelings they identify are generated. The behavior row is ideally made up of those who have participated in the feeling row, unless this is the first group for everyone. Behavior row participants are asked to try to imagine how they might have behaved if the shared experience had happened to them. The result is identification of feelings, physical symptoms, and behavioral responses that are unique to each individual.

STEP 3: INTRODUCTION TO THE OGP TOOLS AND WORKSHEETS

These tools and worksheets are assigned to coincide and enhance the OGP experience. This phase involves one instructional session that can be planned prior to or coinciding with OGP to begin use of the following:

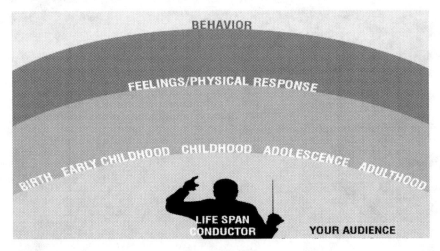

*The G-OM Lifespan Chart*

The G-OM Lifespan Chart (above) is an overview sheet with a timeline that helps the participant pinpoint significant lifespan events (whether positive or negative), the feelings and physical responses associated with each event, and the behaviors enacted when the event occurred. This simple, almost cartoonish, tool appears non-threatening and requires only one-word responses that spontaneously elicit more information. The worksheet has two versions, is an evolving process throughout G-OM, and gives the participant an important role as "conductor" of his/her revealing lifespan history.

### The Level of Intensity Meter

In an image that resembles a carnival gong meter with the hammer representing a disturbing event, the lower portion of the meter represents normal responses from mild to highly intense and the upper gong circle represents an extreme response.

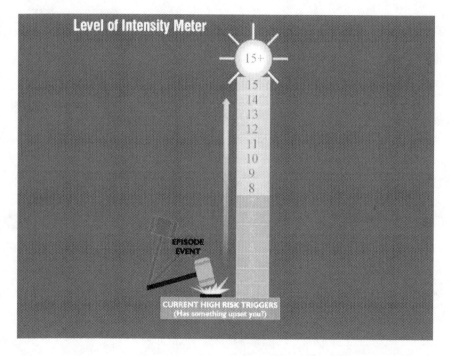

### The Daily Prediction Scale (DPS)

The Daily Prediction Scale (DPS) was developed from the Level of Intensity Meter and is assigned during G-OM behavioral development work. This version requests information about the amount of time spent experiencing the various levels indicated on the meter, particularly the time experienced in an extreme state during each 24-hour period, and whether the old behavior or the new alternative behavior was enacted during the behavioral response. DPS helps to identify high-risk predictors such as persistent disruptive emotional states, the types of triggers that produce them, physical responses that may be health risk alerts, and behavioral responses that could sabotage recovery progress. This tool also measures if there is a reduction in the level of intensity to daily situations that normally generate maladaptive responses, and most importantly, it measures daily progress in developing new responses when extreme states are generated. The DPS demonstrates the individual nature of events and responses that can be indentified within the conceptual and consistent boundaries of this worksheet.

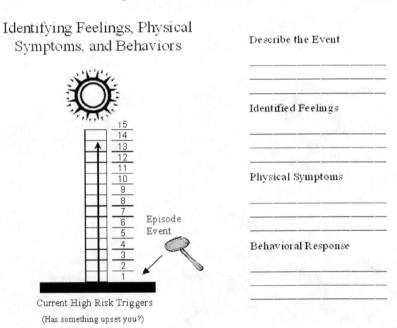

The Memory Episode Dynamic: The MED is both a visual aid that appears as a focal point during the orchestration group process, and a worksheet that is made available after each group session. MED was created to capture and process memory episodes that OGP participants identify during group sessions or worksheet exercises. This valuable clinical tool also represents the circle above the DPS meter; an extreme/pivotal event response to either a current or past experience. Since there is only one experience shared per OGP, and hundreds of experiences to address during the GOM process, this worksheets enables each participant to reveal their most significant life events and determine how they will be further processed beyond the worksheet, whether in group, private session, or otherwise. The worksheet exercise also has a therapeutic benefit. It has a central circle for the vivid details captured in memory that represent the experience, a surrounding circle for the feelings and physical symptoms generated during the experience, and a broader surrounding circle for the behavioral response. The MED is also a replica of the group process, enabling participants to understand that each section of the orchestration group configuration represents a component of pivotal experience. The MED addresses a variety of experiences not limited to trauma. The worksheet has a happy circle face on one side and a sad on the other to be checked. G-OM addresses the full spectrum of experience from joy to suffering; the criteria being the extreme nature of the experience and its persistent intrusion into current life functioning.

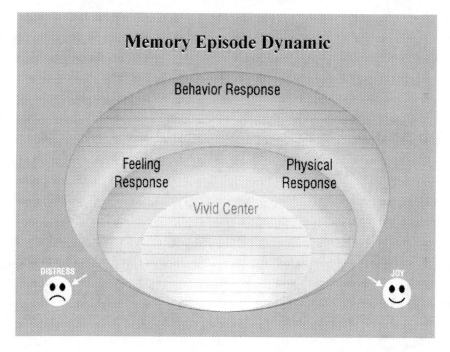

**Group Recorder Worksheets:** The Group Recorder Worksheet (GRW) is a replica of the MED, but has additional space for group process information and serves two purposes. First, the GRW is assigned to one group participant during the OGP to record the experience shared by the soloist. The person chosen can do this task while also participating. The GRW used during OGP has an additional page for recording the responses of each group participant. Because each group process addresses a different pivotal experience and produces an array of individual combinations of feeling/physical symptom/behavior responses shared by each participant, an important record is created that can be translated into clinical documentation. This information is also applied to their worksheet exercises. The data produced provides a window into the consistent dynamic results of the OGP. Second, the GRW is used in small group sessions that revolve around this worksheet.

STEP 4: MONITORING THE SYMPTOMS: PHYSICAL MEMORY = RAPID RESPONSE

The **Daily Prediction Scale (DPS)** is probably the most all-around useful clinical tool of the G-OM and it is assigned daily to monitor responses to current life situations and events. It is brief and to the point. It requires that clients fill it in each day to identify and describe events that produce changes in mood, perceptual and physical changes in mind and body, and the behavioral reaction that results. They rate the level of intensity and duration of their most distressful/excitable/intolerable states and reactions. Daily entries on the DPS facilitate the following:

• Daily practice discriminating low- and high-risk dynamics of the client's experience, and linking behavior to feeling states.

• A thoughtful feeling/behavioral review while completing the DPS that motivates clients to experiment with accountability for new and old behavior.

• Clients establish a self-monitoring ritual.

• The repetitive nature of utilizing the DPS helps to establish new behaviors.

• A journal of progress during treatment that helps clients and therapist identify triggers to repetitive feeling/symptom behavior patterns and record measureable progress.

• A series of completed DPS forms presents snapshots of the clients' current life and can be used to explore immediate issues and stresses, and identify risk.

• DPS responses aid documentation in clinical progress notes and progress toward treatment goals.

The **Daily Prediction Scale** is a clinical self-report tool that helps shape positive behavior, identifies external and internal triggers for high-risk behavior, and provides valuable data for clinical documentation. The DPS is a critical component of the G-OM used to treat PTSD symptoms and SUDs, but it can also be utilized as a stand-alone clinical tool for examining client response to any type of mental health, correctional or other behavior.

## STEP 5: TREATING THE BEHAVIOR WITH ALTERNATIVE BEHAVIORAL STRATEGY PLANNING

The G-OM behavioral planning worksheets are implemented to address the most predominant negative emotional states and problematic behavior patterns identified. Only then can behavioral planning be truly individualized and tailored to address the core issues and high risk actions of each person. During this phase of treatment, other cognitive behavioral approaches and case-management strategies can be utilized within the existing program or as a continuing-care option. G-OM behavioral planning sessions are a collaborative process that begins with an analysis of each identified pattern to determine the skills and abilities that support them. New alternative actions are more successfully adopted when they utilize existing advantages. The prevalent emotional states that have become dependent on certain actions will more readily subside if the new behavior includes cues that can be recognized by the brain as similar. Participants are more motivated when alternative behavioral success is achieved. Otherwise, a reversion to the dependent behavior will occur after a brief period of trying to change. Change is more likely to occur when new behavior becomes more dominant than the old through successful repetition.

## STEP 6: COMPOSING STRATEGIES AND CREATING SOLUTIONS

A workshop session at the conclusion of each week enables participants to discuss and review worksheets, and collaborate on treatment planning and positive alternative behavioral development in a collective environment that stimulates ideas, insight, and a creative approach to TX development. The G-OM Individual Session Questionnaire & Small Work-Group Sessions are described in Chapter 6.

## STEP 7: CONDUCTING A PLAN AND EVALUATING RISK

During the final phase, an Aftercare Planning Session is conducted using the G-OM Aftercare Planning Checklist, and the Potential Toward Relapse Scale (PTRS). The information emerging from the G-OM helps to create an individually tailored treatment plan that addresses the most predominant psychological and physiological distress symptoms and problematic behavior of each person. The investigation phase of G-OM begins with the initial identification of symptoms and behavior. The OGP and its tools are a natural graduation from assessment to treatment when the behavioral action planning stage begins. The entire process provides critical information, measureable results, and leads to a more comprehensive Aftercare Plan and appropriate referral.

STEP 8: A STEP-BY-STEP GUIDE THAT DEMONSTRATES COMPATIBILITY BE-
TWEEN G-OM AND THE 12-STEP PROGRAM

G-OM works within the case-management structure as a foundation of clinical treatment that coincides and contributes to addiction education, and the 12-
Step Program.

STEP 9: THE FINALE: G-OM EXIT QUESTIONNAIRE

*Supportive Research*

An early influence to the theoretical underpinnings of G-OM was the research conducted by Gerald Edelman. Edelman's theory of neuronal group selection (1987, 1989, 1992) describes how we appraise, organize, and reorganize our
subjective experience of the world. The psychoanalytical implications of both
Edelman's theory and a dynamic systems approach to development and change
(Thelen & Smith) are described by Davis (2002) in a clinical case in which deeply ingrained traumatic experience is transformed through positive, new experiences that impact and become integrated within primary consciousness. Davis
addresses the intrinsic principles of selection and self-organization addressed in
Edelman's theory, and the relevance of recognition, adaptive matching, mapping,
and remapping of trajectories of experience, primary emotions, and brain asym-
metry to developmental change. J. Douglas Bremner, director of mental health
research at the Atlanta VA Medical Center and professor at Emory University
and his team were the first to apply brain imaging to the study of PTSD, finding alterations in victims' brain circuits and systems. "This moved PTSD from
being viewed as a psychological disorder to a brain-based disorder," says Bremner. Studies at Emory University that focused on PTSD have found that both the
formation of a memory and the extinction of it seem to require new synapses to
be formed (Ressler, 2008).

CONCLUSION

There is no one path for recovery and no one group therapy approach that will
help each individual. The G-OM and OGP approaches attempt to bridge the here
and now, solution-focused cognitive behavioral approaches with psychodynamic
approaches that focus on the most significant experiences of individual's lives
and their current impact. The approach described in this manual has been an effective tool for many clinicians to help investigate lifespan experiences in order
to identify underlying emotional and behavioral conditions that are a relapse/
recovery risk factor. OGP enhances other group processes in that participants
emerge from it with a better understanding of self and behavior that lends it-

self to further processing in therapy groups or social skills building group approaches. In the future more research on this method will help further evaluate its effectiveness and may better understand the mechanisms of change that have fostered the current level of effectiveness. This approach could be integrated into a variety of clinical settings including the group therapy practice of therapists addressing addictions and trauma-related disorders.

## References

Davis, S.M. (2002). The relevance of Gerald Edelman's Theory of neuronal group selection and nonlinear dynamic systems for psychoanalysis. *Psychoanalytic Inquiry*, 22:814-840.

Gerwe, C.F., & Ziedonis, D. (2007). Using the Orchestration Group Process of the Gerwe – Orchestration Method in Group Therapy for Addiction and Recovery. *Journal of Groups in Addiction and Recovery*, Vols.2(1). US & Canada: The Haworth Press, Inc.

Gerwe, C. F. (2000). Chronic Addiction Relapse Treatment: The Study of the Effectiveness of The High Risk Identification and Prediction Treatment Method, Part I. *The Journal of Substance Abuse Treatment* 19 (1) 415-427.

Gerwe, C. F. (2000). Chronic Addiction Relapse Treatment: The Study of the Effectiveness of The HRIPTM, Part II. *The Journal of Substance Abuse Treatment* 19 (2) 429-438.

Gerwe, C. F. (2000). Chronic Addiction Relapse Treatment: The Study of the Effectiveness of The High Risk Identification and Prediction Treatment Method, Part III. *The Journal of Substance Abuse Treatment* 19 (3) 439-444.

McKensie, M.N. (Summer, 2008) Forever in fear: Unraveling the mysteries of PTSD. *Brain Storms*. Department of Psychiatry and Behavioral Sciences. Emory University.

# CHAPTER 1. INVESTIGATING THE PHENOMENON OF PIVOTAL EXPERIENCE

## STEP 1: G-OM ASSESSMENT OF BEHAVIORAL HEALTH (ABH)

> "When you combine the idea of whistles at night, the presence of a band of gypsies who are on intimate terms with this old Doctor, the fact that we have every reason to believe that the Doctor has an interest in preventing his stepdaughter's marriage, the dying allusion to a band, and finally, the fact that Miss Helen Stoner heard a metallic clang, which might have been caused by one of those metal bars which secured the shutters falling back into their place, I think that there is good ground to think that the mystery may be cleared up along those lines." — Arthur Conan Doyle, Sherlock Holmes in "The Adventure of the Speckled Band," *The Adventures of Sherlock Holmes*

From the time we are born, we come into the world with genes that determine how we look and even how we behave to a certain degree. We can inherit a predisposition toward conditions that affect our physical and mental health, and physical and mental abilities that influence our level of intelligence and natural attributes. At birth, we enter an environment in which we learn from what we are taught, what we observe, and what we experience. During each stage of development, progress can be measured by stage guidelines developed over decades of clinical research. Both heredity and environment (nature and nurture) are the primary recognized influences that shape each person from childhood into adulthood.

In each life history, however, there is the possibility for a third dimension of influence. The type of experiences that transcend the norm and/or exceed the boundaries of what we can endure; experiences that have a life-altering impact that can affect perception of self, others, and even change our perception of the world in which we live. The power of pivotal experience in the life course of an individual is at the foundation of G-OM and the assessment instruments and worksheet tools produced during its development.

The Gerwe Assessment for Behavioral Health (ABH), found at the conclusion of this chapter, was developed over years of clinical work that focused on the nature and role of pivotal experiences that continued to impact the lives of individuals suffering chronic behavioral and addictive disorders. This 16-question assessment tool was created to identify the most distressful current emotional states of each person, the associated physical and behavioral reactions generated when these states are triggered, and to identify their approximate origin. This G-OM instrument would be ineffective if the type of experiences described here were not set apart from the norm. The extreme *novel* nature of pivotal experiences makes it possible to identify them because they are recorded differently in the neuronal structure of the brain and in physical memory, and are represented by the feelings, physical symptoms, and behavioral patterns that were created at their origin. If they continue to hold power over the person who experienced them, they can be accessed through this feelings/symptoms/behavior portal and investigated further to determine the best course of action for treatment. The ABH is better understood when the path toward its development is reviewed in this chapter.

NOVEL EXPERIENCE

**What is novel experience?** A dictionary definition describes novel as a new kind, or nature, strange, hitherto unknown: beyond the norm and into another realm. In nature, novel events often determine subtle or dramatic shifts in the environment. Catastrophic changes in atmosphere and terrain can impact food and water supply to wildlife. Changes in species occur when it becomes necessary to survive in conditions that are dramatically different than they were prior to the event or series of events. In humans, populations have migrated to new territories and lands when the familiar becomes a strange and impossible place in which to exist. Human behavior can change on a grand scale when a people find themselves in the midst of extreme novel experiences, such as war and other forms of disaster, when the behavior previously developed to that point in time does not suffice to ensure survival.

When a distinct change in behavior occurs and new behavior emerges in response to novel events, it will continue if proven to be effective. Newly constructed behavior can help sustain an individual or group in a new norm that, in a sense, becomes a new reality. If the behavior produces negative consequences, the life direction of that individual or group will be adversely affected if the behavior continues to be repeated and continues to evolve. Intervention can be difficult and ineffective unless the behavioral condition is fully understood in relation to its survival origin.

When the behavioral condition originates and evolves during childhood as a result of extreme experience/s, it can impact neurological development as it becomes an entrenched and encoded formulated response within the still-developing brain, and it can continue to evolve in scope and dimension within the personality and behavior of the child. Neuroscience research and advanced neuro-imaging technologies have opened a new world of exploration into the intricate and complex inter-workings of the human body and brain. Studies investigating the role of novel experience and its impact on the neurological development of the adolescent brain have indicated a correlation between novelty and high-risk behavior. G-OM research for over two decades has been investigating the role of novel/pivotal experience in relation to trauma-related symptoms that produce highly intense to extreme emotional states, associated high-risk behavior, and a propensity toward addictive disorders. The prevalence of unresolved pivotal childhood experiences in these cases, and their compounding effect on later experiences of this nature helps to explain the difficulty that some people have recovering from situations that others are able to overcome. The identification of conditions stemming from experiences that repeatedly disrupt current functioning helps to provide a basis for more intensified treatment approaches that address the complexity of these disorders. ABH addresses the need for assessment that identifies these conditions at the earliest possible phase of treatment so that effective treatment planning can be implemented.

WHY INVESTIGATE AND IDENTIFY PIVOTAL EXPERIENCES FROM THE PAST?

When a child has an experience that generates *feelings* and *physical symptoms* that escalate to a level of emotional and physical intensity that is intolerable for the child, the extreme state of distress/arousal can overwhelm the child's ability to think and act rationally. When recalled, these episodes are often described in this way: "I could not stand it another minute." "I felt like I was going to die." Whether described as intolerable distress/suffering, or excruciating arousal/excitement, the level of intensity appears to be the transforming catalyst that generates a behavioral response at the point when the bearable becomes unbearable and the need for relief predominates.

The newly constructed behavior/s, if effective, is recognized by the brain as the solution to the unprecedented internal crisis produced by the event. If the feeling/physical-symptom state produced by the experience is once again triggered by a similar type of experience, or by sensory stimuli associated with the original episode, the child will feel impulsively compelled to repeat the behavior, even if the behavior has negative consequences. If the behavior continues to evolve over time, the pattern is strengthened while the negative consequences accumulate and interfere with normal positive development.

CASE EXAMPLE

Johnny, age four, while running through the living room chasing the family cat, bumps into a small table knocking over his mother's treasured lamp. Mother hears the noise and enters the room. Upon seeing the broken lamp, her facial expression changes reflecting anger. Johnny has never before seen this expression and he begins to feel intense fear. The fear escalates when his mother begins to speak in a harsh tone. Johnny immediately begins to experience the physical symptoms of raised body temperature, trembling, sweaty palms, and pressure to urinate. He tries but cannot stop the trembling in his legs and his lower lip. He finds it increasingly difficult to swallow. Johnny has never seen his mother so upset. She cries, "Johnny, did you do this? Did you break my beautiful lamp?"

Without thinking, Johnny blurts out, "I didn't do it!" Pointing toward the corner of the room where the cat is hiding, he exclaims, "The cat did it!" Mother quickly looks toward the cat and fiercely scolds the creature and puts him outside. Johnny feels immediate relief. The lie worked. The cat was blamed. Although Johnny felt a guilty about what he had done, the lie remained secret. He tried to alleviate his negative feelings by making a promise to himself to never lie to his mother again. But the next time Johnny got into trouble and was confronted by his mother, the same intense fear and physical symptoms were re-triggered and he lied again, blaming someone else for what he had done. Johnny's negative self-perception grew as the pattern evolved over time.

Johnny later joined the military during a time of war and became involved in a combat situation. During one horrific episode, he made a strategic error that cost the life of a fellow soldier. He was able to cover-up his mistake and blame enemy forces. But he could not resolve the accumulated bad feelings he had about himself after the war. He became dependent on alcohol to alleviate his guilt. He lied and covered up his drinking until it cost him his marriage and job. He could not sustain periods of sobriety because he could not endure the negative emotions and repetitive dishonesty that continued to plague him. He declined in health and morale and his addiction to alcohol became chronic.

BREAKING DOWN PIVOTAL EXPERIENCE INTO IDENTIFIABLE COMPONENTS

**Feeling Response**: The feeling response can encompass a variety of feelings such as anger, shame, fear, sadness, loneliness, etc. The nature of these feelings, while important, is not as relevant to this dynamic as the level of intensity. Even positive feelings can escalate when physical symptoms are generated and individual perception is involved. Like a percolating coffeepot, feelings, physical symptoms, and perception can impact each other in a percolating dynamic that merges them together as the intensity increases and reaches a point of transformation at the most extreme level.

**Physical Response**: Physical symptoms are generated as feelings intensify. For example, rapid heartbeat, difficulty breathing, trembling, changes in body temperature, loss of body fluids, nausea, etc. can produce a state of physical discomfort that intensifies the feelings generated and sometimes produces additional feelings. Physical symptoms are unique to each individual and can also be produced by positive feelings such as anticipation, excitement, exhilaration. At the most extreme level, even pleasurable feeling/symptom reactions can produce behavior that is problematic. The naturalist, W. H. Hudson, in 1916, provides an example in his classic novel, *Green Mansions*. From the following glorious experience, his character developed an obsession for solitude that almost cost him his life.

> As I crossed the savannah I played with this fancy; but when I reached the ridgy domain, the fancy changed to a feeling so keen that it pierced to my heart, and was like pain in its intensity, causing tears to rush to my eyes. And caring not in that solitude to disguise my feelings from myself, and from the wide heaven that looked down and saw me—for this is the sweetest thing that solitude has for us, that we are free in it, and no convention holds us — I dropped to my knees and kissed the stony ground, then casting up my eyes, thanked the Author of my being for the gift of that wild forest, those green mansions where I had found so great a happiness.

This description not only exemplifies the feelings and physical reaction that can happen during an escalating state of euphoria, it also provides an example of how the associated behavior of seeking solitude (which in this case became an obsession), became so compelling.

**Perception**: A child's perception of an experience can dramatically impact the level of intensity. Children vary greatly in how they individually respond to situations. Perception can be affected by the age of the child, circumstances surrounding the experience, and what is happening within the experience. Perception is influenced by hereditary and environmental factors, and the unique imagination of the child. Perception of the event is also a key factor in the constructed behavioral response. — Nobel Laureate Gerald Edelman writes:

> When I started to study how synapses work and how messages come in from the outside world, it became clear to me that the diversity of the brain is even staggeringly larger than its anatomical complexity. It is the most diverse object that I could think of, except an evolutionary jungle. Then I

was naturally prompted to look at perceptual phenomena as perhaps the most simple early function of the higher brain. And when I looked at that, it became clear that your brain *constructs.* There's no avoiding that, in some deep cases, it constructs. It doesn't mirror.

Whether or not the child's perception of the event is accurate, the effect is the same if the intensity level escalates to extreme. The child's perception becomes the reality in relation to behavioral construction and memory of the event. Vivid recollections of pivotal experiences often include descriptions of frightening experiences involving people, places and/or images that were distorted to some degree by the perception and imagination of the child. The patterns that emerge from them, however, are frighteningly real.

**Case example:** Stuart, a 32-year-old white male in treatment for cocaine dependence, volunteered to share an experience during OGP that he said occurred when he was approximately 8-years old. He began by sharing two important pieces of background information:

1) Two days before the episode occurred, Stuart's mother informed him and his father that their family physician had died of a heart attack. Stuart had just seen the doctor and could not believe that he had died so suddenly. Stuart became preoccupied with how this could have happened.

2) The day of the episode, Stuart's older brother told him a scary story about an "orange monkey-man," he ominously warned, "that could slip his hand through the window at night and snatch your eyeballs out."

With these two incidents fresh in his mind, Stuart went to bed that night in his upstairs bedroom. He slept on a lower bunk of a bunk bed that was situated near a window. His sister occupied the upper bunk.

**Stuart's described vivid memory:** "I was in a deep sleep when I was awakened by something pulling on my eyelashes. It was dark. I remember seeing the hall light through the open bedroom door, and looking down at my red bedspread. I could see no one else in the room. My immediate thought was that the orange monkey-man had reached through the window to get me. My next thought was that I was going to have a heart attack and die."

**Stuart's described feeling response:** "I felt shocked and scared to death, wondering if I was going to die."

**Stuart's described physical symptom response:** "I had heart palpitations due to fear of the eyeball snatcher man, and being convinced that I was going to have a heart attack. I could feel my heart racing and had shortness of breath that worsened until I was gasping for air."

**Stuart's described behavioral response:** "I started screaming, jumped from the bed and ran to my parents. My mother was downstairs. My sister awoke and became hysterical. My brother came out from under the bed in response to her hysteria. He had been hiding there and had reached up and pulled on my eyelashes like the monkey-man he had told me about that day. My sister told on my brother as I hysterically told my mother that I was having a heart attack. She tried to calm me down and my father tried to help her convince me that I was not about to die. I was not convinced and could only think of our doctor—he could not even predict or prevent his own death from a heart attack.

"After a lengthy period of trying to assure me that I wasn't dying, my parents insisted that I return to bed and scolded my brother for what he had done. Although my heart rate had once again returned to normal, I could not sleep, and was convinced that my heart would start palpitating again if something came to my window. I was still worried about the window, despite knowing that my brother had tricked me. I was worried that something would happen again. My breathing was still irregular. By the next day, I was determined to convince my parents that something was wrong with my heart. They took me to a doctor. He tried to assure me that I had not had a heart attack and that I was not going to have one. I was not convinced.

"The next night, I could not sleep. I continued to worry about another incident. This lack of sleep went on for weeks. I finally figured out a way to position my neck on a rolled-up pillow in such a way as to affect my breathing. With my breathing altered, I could then go to sleep. I think I was cutting off oxygen to my brain. Essentially, I had assessed and diagnosed my own condition and came up with a solution. This did not relieve my anxiety, but it did help me sleep."

Stuart's behavioral response to his extreme state of panic was to take control of the situation after trying desperately to convince others to listen to him. When they did listen to him and try to help him, he did not trust their conclusions. He was convinced that he was not safe in his bedroom at night and that he was going to die. When his siblings made fun of him, he pretended to ignore them while trying desperately to gain control of his feelings of fear, anger and humiliation. Stuart's behavioral response to this experience resulted in obsessive attempts to control his fear of death and dying, his sleeplessness, and to prevent feelings of powerlessness, humiliation, and a growing lack of security and trust.

After the episode, Stuart continued to believe that he had a heart condition. He continued to devise breathing techniques to help him sleep. He developed a serious sleep disorder; he could put himself to sleep, but his sleep continued to be restless and he awoke easily at the slightest sound or movement. He began devising strategic methods of prevention by securing his room, moving his bed, checking the windows, and being more watchful. With every slight ailment, he diagnosed his own condition and devised his own treatments and remedies. He became more demanding of his parents' attention and continually questioned them about his concerns. His concerns were primarily focused on home security and health issues. When he wanted answers to his questions, he could be relentless. He stated, "I was never satisfied." If he was not satisfied with the answers given in response to his questions, he stubbornly debated. Because he loved his parents, he tempered his inclination to argue too aggressively. This politeness in manner was incorporated into his developing pattern of behavior, which carried over into every area of his life. In school he was a good student, but debated just as relentlessly with his teachers. After graduation, he went into the family business in order to remain close to his parents. Fear of his own death extended to them as he began to obsess about their death. He married and started a family and obsessed about losing his wife and children. He described his family as essential to his well-being. Loss of family, separation, or even lack of communication with family members triggered him into a state of panic.

Stuart stated that his drug use began in his teens with alcohol and pot. Later, in his late twenties, he began using cocaine as a self-prescribed medication. He said it was initially beneficial in relieving what he described as a constant state of tension, fear, anxiety, and it made him feel more in control and less fearful. As his addiction progressed, he became nervous and paranoid and increasingly demanding and argumentative. He could no longer temper his verbal aggression as his behavior and panic attacks spiraled out of control. He began stealing money from the business to support his cocaine addiction. His wife threatened to leave him and take the children. His father had him arrested when family intervention failed. He entered treatment as a condition of his probation.

**Time Factor:** Stuart's case provides an example of the power of perception. Time is another important factor. Each second, moment, hour the child endures an extreme state, the level of intensity increases stimulation of neural circuitry influencing synaptic activity in the brain. When physical action (external behavioral relief) is not possible, mental activity increases in an effort to find a solution. An intolerable/excruciating state that is extended for any length of time due to an inability to escape the situation or find effective relief can produce a time-related sequence of internal thought processes and actions that form an internal behavioral response. As the child desperately and instinctively *constructs* behavioral actions to achieve regulation, the time it takes and the sequence of these actions will be replicated if the state is once again triggered. Pivotal experiences characterized by entrapment, near-suffocation, drowning, physical confinement, torture, and even extended periods of extreme excitement/anticipation without relief can result in a sequence of behaviors that replicates the sequence as the pattern evolves. Internal actions such as strategic thinking, planning, praying, wishing, imagining, fantasizing, and various forms of detachment, are often constructed when external actions are not possible.

**Need, Desire, and Intention:** During an extreme state of suffering or excitement, a child's ability to make rationale judgments can diminish. Intention and decisive action are overwhelmed by desperation and the need for relief. Experiences that produce an extreme level of suffering can also produce patterns of behavior constructed to prevent re-occurrence. Experiences that produce extreme levels of joy/exhilaration/arousal can produce patterns of behavior constructed to achieve reoccurrence of the extremely pleasurable state. These dual patterns can develop in the immediate aftermath of pivotal experiences and develop simultaneously. Both are driven by desperate need and desire that can overwhelm rational thinking. Deliberate intention is often mistakenly assumed to be the driving force in behaviors stemming from pivotal experiences, when in reality they are driven by a much more powerful dynamic. While intention can be a factor at some point in pattern development, the primary motivating factors in these behaviors are need and/or desire that can become so powerfully intense, it overtakes the child's ability to resist or stop the behavior.

**Duel-Pattern Development:** Behavior patterns that include prevention patterns can become an obsessive preoccupation for the child if similar situations continue to occur, or the child fears a re-occurrence of the situation/event. This duel dynamic is more likely to occur in situations where family dysfunction or various kinds of repeated abuse are prevalent.

Obsessive pre-occupation can also occur in children with dual patterns related to extreme states of arousal/excitement/euphoria. This dual-dynamic can result in an obsessive desire to replicate the pleasurable feeling and devise ways of extending the replicated state as long as possible when it is re-produced. This is particularly true of children who experience little happiness or joy in their normal lives. A pattern of high-risk behavior related to euphoria can develop when the child's desire for pleasure replication continues to intensify. A suffering child is more likely to develop a desperate need to have the euphoric feeling again, once experienced.

This compounded dynamic advances the pattern in scope, dimension, and complexity. Dual patterns that engage the child in obsessive preoccupation are more likely to develop into obsessive/compulsive disorders. Obsessive preoccupation involving pornographic or violent images, various forms of sexual experimentation, such as prepubescent masturbation, are linked to episodes involving extreme states of arousal. Early childhood phenomenal experiences of spiritual bliss have been studied by researchers investigating obsessive patterns of religious zeal in adults. Whether the pattern of behavior has positive appearing characteristics or negative, it is the repetitive and obsessive nature of the patterns that is the problematic factor. Once a pattern is established and evolves over time, the behavior/s can infiltrate every aspect of a person's life, influence relationship choices, career choices, and can be hidden or camouflaged. And although traumatic experiences command more clinical focus in relation to high-risk patterns of behavior, patterns stemming from extreme arousal states should demand more attention. Russian writer, Fyodor Dostoevsky provides a remarkable example of the dangers involved in replicating an extreme state of bliss in his description of the feelings he experienced before having an epileptic seizure. In 1867, writing to the critic Nikolai Strakhov, he explained,

> For a few moments before the fit, I experience a feeling of happiness such as it is quite impossible to imagine in a normal state and which other people have no idea of. I feel in harmony with myself and the whole world, and this feeling is so strange and so delightful that for a few seconds of such bliss one would gladly give up ten years of one's life, if not one's whole life.

Much has been written about the deprivation Dostoevsky suffered during his youth. His father was known to be a cruel and abusive man and was the subject of his great novel, The Brothers Karamazov. As a youth he was sent to university, and living on a mere pittance, he spent evenings in a coffee shop where he and a group of friends were arrested for expressing revolutionary ideas. Incarcerated and sentenced to death, he suffered terribly before the execution was canceled at the last minute. His experiences were translated into brilliant novels that brought financial income lost in gambling and other high-risk behavior. Some of his greatest masterpieces were written to appease creditors. His genius was found in his understanding of suffering and its impact on human behavior. But his intense desire for the "feeling of happiness" was such that he refused to take medication to prevent his severe epileptic seizures (the "fit" he describes above) that often left him incapacitated for days.

**Pattern Identification:** Pivotal experiences, even when horrific, are in a sense like a new discovery; a powerful phenomenon that accesses a person's most basic instinctual drives and behavior. Behavioral construction that occurs under the most extreme conditions utilizes natural ability and generates spontaneous innovation. The behavioral result not only becomes the solution for the immediate situation, but provides a solution for future situations that arouse and/or endanger us. Like the term *second nature*, these behaviors emerge as a temporary salvation that, when repeated, can also have the power to sabotage a person's life. But they also hold within them the key to their undoing. Treatment of conditions and behavior stemming from pivotal experiences that are powerfully disrupting current life must first begin with their identification. So, the first step in G-OM is to assign the **Assessment for Behavioral Health (ABH)** designed to initiate this investigation.

## THE G-OM ASSESSMENT QUESTIONNAIRE FOR BEHAVIORAL HEALTH (ABH)

1. At present, during a 24-hour period of time, in a typical day, which of the following "feelings" seem to occur to you the *most* often?

    (a) anger             (d) shame

    (b) fear              (e) loneliness

    (c) sadness

2. List below the physical symptoms that occur in your body when you experience the feeling/s you identified. (For example: shallow breathing, nausea, rapid heartbeat, tight neck and shoulders, headache, or others.

 

 

 

3. Approximately what percentage, or how much of the time, in a typical day, do you feel this way?

    (a) Less than 25%     (d) 75%

    (b) 25%             (e) 100%

    (c) 50%

4. When you experience the feeling/s and physical symptoms you identified, do you think of . . .

    (a) The present        (d) The present and the past

    (b) The past           (e) The present and the future

    (c) The future

5. Can you remember the age period when you first experienced the feeling you identified — your first memory of this feeling?

    (a) Ages 1 thru 5      (d) Ages 21 thru 40

    (b) Ages 6 thru 12     (e) Ages 41 thru 80

    (c) Ages 13 thru 20

6. When you experience the feeling you identified, which of the following behaviors is most likely to occur? (Circle all that apply.)

    (a) Isolating, withdrawal, avoidance

    (b) Acting, pretending, hiding feelings

    (c) Verbal aggression, verbal abuse

    (d) Physical aggression, physical abuse, violent action

    (e) None of the above

7. When you experience the feeling you identified, which of the following behaviors is most likely to occur? (Circle all that apply.)

    (a) Any form of self abuse

    (b) A behavior that you believe to be dishonest

    (c) High risk behaviors, life threatening behaviors

    (d) Destruction of objects, property, possessions

    (e) None of the above

8. When you experience the feeling you identified, which of the following behaviors is most likely to occur?

    (a) Pre-occupation with food

    (b) Pre-occupation with money

    (c) Pre-occupation with sex

    (d) Pre-occupation with control

    (e) None of the above

9. When you experience the feeling you identified, which of the following behaviors is most likely to occur? (Circle all that apply.)

    (a) Pre-occupation with suicide

    (b) Pre-occupation with fire, explosives, weapons

    (c) Pre-occupation with collecting, hiding, hoarding objects

    (d) Pre-occupation with a person, celebrity, group, place

    (e) None of the above

10. When you experience the feeling you identified, which of the following behaviors is most likely to occur? (Circle all that apply.)

    (a) Fantasizing about death

    (b) Fantasizing about revenge, retaliation

    (c) Fantasizing about sex, power

    (d) Fantasizing about being another person, being in a different place, being in a different circumstance

    (e) None of the above

11. When you experience the feeling you identified, which of the following behaviors is most likely to occur? (Circle all that apply.)

    (a) Adjusting your behavior to become the center of attention

    (b) Adjusting your behavior to avoid the attention of others

    (c) Adjusting your behavior to please, manipulate, control others

    (d) Adjusting your behavior to anger others

    (e) None of the above

12. When you experience the feeling you identified, which of the following behaviors is most likely to occur? (Circle all that apply.)

    (a) Attempts to "hide" in a specific place or places

    (b) Attempts to run, escape from a situation

    (c) Attempts to disguise your appearance in some way

    (d) Attempts to control a situation, a place, a group

(e) None of the above

13. If you identified a behavior or behaviors that have developed into a repetitive pattern in relation to the feelings you identified, mark the age period in which this combination first occurred?

    (a) Ages 1 thru 5

    (b) Ages 6 thru 12

    (c) Ages 13 thru 20

    (d) Ages 21 thru 40

    (e) Ages 41 thru 80

14. Was this pattern or patterns of behavior in existence . . .

    (a) Prior to age 5 with no use of mood-altering substances

    (b) Prior to age 12 with no use of mood-altering substances

    (c) Prior to first use of mood-altering substances

    (d) Prior to addictive use of mood-altering substances

    (e) Began with first use or during addiction to mood-altering substances

15. Have you ever attempted to . . .

    (a) Change the behavior or behaviors

    (b) Stop the behavior or behaviors

    (c) Hide the behavior or behaviors

    (d) Limit the behavior or behaviors

    (e) None of the above

16. Has the feeling/behavior combination or combinations you identified ever created...

    (a) A problem in your life

    (b) Occasional problems in your life

    (c) Many problems in your life

    (d) Continuous problems in your life

    (e) None of the above

G-OM-ABH TEMPLATE SUMMARY
(Circle the answers identified on the ABH Questionnaire)

Name:_____ _____     Date:_____

Counselor:_____

1. At present, during a 24-hour period of time in a typical day, I feel:
   (anger)     (fear)     (sadness)     (shame)     (loneliness)

2. Physical symptoms that occur with the identified feeling/s are:

   _____

   _____

3. At present, during a 24-hour period of time in a typical day, I experience the feelings and physical symptoms identified :
   (less than 25%)     (25%)     (50%)     (75%)     (100% of the time)

4. When I experience the feeling/s _____, and/or the physical symptoms _____, I think of the:
   ( present)     (past)     (future)     (present & past)     (present & future)

5. My first memory of this feeling/symptoms was at age:
   (1–5)     (6– 12)     (13–20)     (21–40)     (41–80)

6. When I experience the feeling/symptoms,

   [a] I am likely to: (isolate) (withdraw) (avoid) (become an actor) (pretend) (hide feelings) (be verbally aggressive) (be verbally abusive) (be physically aggressive) (be physically abusive) (be violent) (engage in a form of self abuse) (become dishonest) (engage in high risk behaviors) (engage in life threatening behaviors) (destroy objects) (destroy property) (destroy possessions)

   [b] I believe I do not engage in behaviors related to (avoidance).

   [c] I believe I do not engage in behaviors related to physical aggression.

7. When I experience the feeling/symptoms,

   [a] I become pre-occupied with: (food) (money) (sex) (control) (suicide) (fire) (explosives) (weapons)    (collecting things) (hiding things) (hoarding objects) (a person) (a celebrity) (a group) (a place)

   [b] I believe I do not become (excessively concerned) (distracted) (preoccupied with specific thoughts or behaviors)

8. When I experience the feeling/symptoms,

   [a] I fantasize about: (death) (revenge) (retaliation) (sex) (power)

(being another person) (being in a different place) (being in a different circumstance)

[b] I believe I do not engage in: (fanaticizing or daydreaming about changing my identity) (my circumstances) (verbal or physical aggression) (events involving sex) (power)

9. When I experience the feeling/symptoms,

[a] I adjust my behavior to: (become the center of attention) (avoid the attention of others) (please others) (manipulate others) (control others) (anger others)

[b] I believe I do not adjust my behavior to (affect others)

10. When I experience the feeling/symptoms,

[a] I attempt to: (hide in a specific place or places) (run from a situation) (escape from a situation) (disguise myself in some way) (control a situation) (control a place) (control a group)

[b] I believe I do not attempt to (avoid) (control a situation).

11. The age in my life when the feelings, physical symptoms, and the above behavior pattern(s) first occurred was:

(ages 1–5) (ages 6–12) (ages 13–20) (ages 21–40) (ages 41–80)

12. This pattern/these patterns of behavior were in existence:

(prior to age 5 with no use of mood-altering substances)

(prior to age 12 with no use of mood-altering substances)

(prior to first use of mood-altering substances)

(prior to addictive use of mood-altering substances)

(began or coincided with first use and onset of addiction to mood-altering substances)

13. I have attempted to:

[a] (Change the behavior or behaviors)

(Stop the behavior or behaviors)

(Hide the behavior or behaviors)

(Limit the behavior or behaviors)

[b] I believe I have not attempted to (change) (stop) (hide) (limit my behavior(s)

14. The feeling/symptom/ behavior combination(s) identified have created:

(a problem in my life) (occasional problems in my life) (many problems in my life) (continuous problems in my life) (no problems in my life)

\* \* \*

## G-OM-ABH Template **Summarized Example** #1

Name: **John D.**    Date: Jan. 20, 2004___    Counselor: **David C.**

1. At present, during a 24-hour period of time in a typical day, I feel:    (fear)
2. The physical symptoms that occur when I feel fear are: (headache)
3. I feel this combination:  (50%) of the time
4. When I feel fear, I think of the (past)
5. My first memory of this fear was during the age period age: (6 thru 12)
6. When I experience (fear) and (headaches), I am likely to: (become an actor) (pretend) (hide feelings) (be verbally aggressive) (be verbally abusive) (be physically aggressive) (be physically abusive)(be violent) (engage in a form of self-abuse) (be dishonest) (engage in high risk behaviors) (engage in life threatening behaviors) (destroy objects) (destroy property) (destroy possessions).
7. I become pre-occupied with: (money) (sex) (weapons) (collecting) (hiding) (hoarding objects) (a person) (a celebrity) (a place).
8. I fantasize about: (death) (revenge) (retaliation) (sex) (power) (being another person) (being in a different place) (being in a different circumstance).
9. I adjust my behavior to: (become the center of attention) (avoid the attention of others) (anger others).
10. I attempt to: (run from a situation) (escape from a situation) (control a situation) (control a place) (control a group)
11. The age in my life when (fear) and (headaches) and the identified behavior first occurred was the age period (6 thru 12)
12. This pattern of behavior was in existence: (prior to age 12 with no use of mood-altering substances)
13. I have attempted to: (change the behaviors) (limit the behaviors)
14. The feeling/physical symptom/behavior have caused: (a problem in my life)

G-OM-ABH Template Summarized Example #2

Name: Jane D.    Date: Feb. 20, 2005___    Counselor: **David C.**

1. At present, during a 24-hour period of time in a typical day, I feel:

(loneliness) (25%) of the time.

2. The physical symptoms that occur when I feel loneliness are: (headache and tight neck and shoulders, heart beats uneven)

3. I feel this combination (25%) of the time.

4. When I feel loneliness and the identified physical symptoms, I think of the: (past)

5. My first memory of this fear was during the age period age: (13 thru 20)

6. When I experience (fear) (headache, tightness in neck and shoulders, uneven heartbeat), I am likely to: (become an actor) (pretend) (hide feelings) (become dishonest).

7. I become pre-occupied with: (money).

8. I fantasize about: (sex) (power).

9. I adjust my behavior to: (please others) (manipulate others) (control others).

10. I attempt to: (control a situation) (control a place) (control a group).

11. The age in my life when (fear) and (headaches) and the identified behavior first occurred was the age period (13 thru 20).

12. This pattern of behavior was in existence: (prior to first use of mood-altering substances)

13. I have attempted to: (change the behaviors)

14. The feeling/physical symptom/behavior have caused: (a problem in my life)

* * *

## ADVANTAGES OF THE ABH

Clients select detailed descriptions of unhealthy behavior responses that are triggered by specific negative emotional states. A summary of selected behavior patterns can indicate problem areas concerning potential for: violence, avoidance, compulsive thinking and behavior, fantasy, and difficulty with internal controls.

ABH behavioral terminology translates client responses into language that can justify ASAM levels of treatment and decisions for length of stay.

Behavioral terminology also assists the therapist with individualizing behavioral treatment plans: identifying initial problem lists as well as goals.

Response to the ABH questionnaire can be manually translated into "I" statements that connect the client's predominant negative feeling state with past and current behavior patterns. When clients are invited to confirm, disagree with, re-word or elaborate their ABH self-descriptions during group or individual sessions, issues worth exploring are effectively prioritized.

# References

Chambers, R., Taylor, J., & Potenza, M. (2003). Developmental neurocircuitry of motiva-tion in adolescence: A critical period of addiction vulnerability. American Journal of Psychiatry, 60(6):1041-1052.

Dostoyevsky, F. (1952). The Brothers Karamazov. (C. Garnet, Trans.) Originally published 1880. Chicago, Il: William Benton.

Edelman, G.M. (Feb. 1995). Neural Darwinism: selection and reentrant signaling in higher brain function. Neuron,10 (2): 115-25. New York: Neurosciences Institute.

Hoffman, E. (1992). Visions of Innocence: Spiritual and Inspirational Experiences of Childhood. Boston/New York: Shambhala.

Levy, S. (May 2, 1994). "Annals of Science: Dr. Edelman's Brain." The New Yorker.

Magarshack, D. (1955). Introduction In (Trans): Fyodor Dostoyevsky, The Idiot. Middlesex, England, Penguin Books.

W. H. (William Henry). Green Mansions. First published as Green Mansions: A Romance of the Tropical Forest, New York, G.P. Putnam's Sons; London, Duckworth & Co., 1904. 2 p. l., 315, [1] p. 20 cm. LoC 05-4148, LC CALL NUMBER: PZ3.H8697 Gr.

# CHAPTER 2. EXPLORING THE ORIGIN AND PATH OF THE CORE PROBLEM

## STEP 2: THE ORCHESTRATION GROUP PROCESS (OGP)

> "Do you remember what Darwin says about music? He claims that the power of producing and appreciating it existed among the human race long before the power of speech was arrived at. Perhaps that is why we are so subtly influenced by it. There are vague memories in our souls of those misty centuries when the world was in its childhood." — Arthur Conan Doyle. Holmes speaking to Watson in A Study In Scarlet.

The Gerwe Orchestration Method (G-OM) group therapy approach blends cognitive behavioral therapy and psychodynamic approaches to target dysfunctional addictive behaviors that originated during pivotal developmental experiences and continued to evolve through repetition and linkage with the addiction. The Orchestration Group Process (OGP) is the cornerstone of G-OM and provides a method to better understand the relationship of current behaviors and previous pivotal life experiences. The OGP approach has been successfully integrated into the addiction group therapy in a variety of settings with or without the full use of the other components of the G-OM method, including intensive outpatient, military, and criminal justice settings. The following describes the OGP method and its historical roots.

OGP is firmly grounded in many therapy traditions such as CBT, psychodynamics, psychodrama, Gestalt, and even Tavistock group process techniques. One of the great influencers of this clinical work, Dr. Edward J. Khantzian, has summarized well a similar perspective: "I have always felt that there are too many arbitrary boundaries between paradigms and that astute clinicians can see the overlap and common elements to effective treatments. In fact much of CBT is totally consistent with ego (structural) psychology which derives from psychoanalytic theory/practice. Freud and his followers, with their early emphasis on drive (i.e., what drives the engine) theory, needed to then explain what controlled and regulated the engine, thus structural or ego theory had to evolve, the ego being the mediator between the inner terrain and external reality. In addition to all the troubles with recognizing and expressing feelings, patients with SUDs have major difficulty regulating their behaviors, particularly their deficits in self-care (the inability to perceive and anticipate danger), a major factor that predisposes a person to become involved in addictive behaviors (Khantzian, personal communication 2006)."

Beyond the psychoanalytic approach, historically, the psychodrama approach developed by Moreno in the 30's and 40's created a forum in which participants in assigned roles were encouraged to "emote" their responses during re-enactment of past experience in order to achieve "catharsis" (Moreno 1946/1972). The Gestalt Tradition (Feder & Ronall, 2000) developed by Fritz Perls and others that followed also assigned roles and relied heavily on improvisation to produce catharsis, new awareness, and bring about change (Perls, 1969). G-OM is similar in that roles are assigned during the Orchestration Group Process (OGP), but differs in that participants move through the emotional stage of re-exploring past experience by an analytical process of identifying and separating into components their feelings and physical symptoms so that the primary goal of moving forward to the stage of identifying behavioral responses and patterns is not hampered. OGP teaches participants how to be "fully there" for one another and demonstrates that life experiences can be positively readdressed in a way that alleviates and diminishes the suffering that continues to result from them. Palmer (1990) writes, "To suffer with another person does not mean to drown oneself in the other's suffering; that would be as foolish as jumping in the pool to save a sinking swimmer only to drown oneself. More to the point, I doubt that it is even possible to enter fully into another person's pain, for suffering is a profoundly solitary experience. To suffer with another person means to be there in whatever way possible, to share the circumstances of another's life as much as one can— not to add to the world's pool of suffering, but to gain intimate understanding of what the other requires. What we usually learn, once we are there, is that there is no *fix* for the person who suffers, only the slow and painful process of walking through the suffering to whatever lies on the other side. Once there, we learn that being there is the best we can do, being there not as a cure but as a companion to the person who suffers on his or her slow journey. There is no arm's-length *solution* for suffering, and people who offer such only add to the pain. But there is comfort and even healing in the presence of people who know how to be with others, how to fully be there."

Similar to psychodrama, the OGP approach assigns roles to each participant and also an assigned placement in the group structure. The group is structured like an orchestra with most participants sitting in one of two rows in semi-circles facing the facilitator "conductor" and discloser "soloist." The first row is the feeling / physical symptom row. The second row is the behavior row. The facilitator "conductor" focuses the group on the story of the "soloist," and the entire group process revolves around one shared experience per-group while each participant shares his/her response to the experience presented. OGP relies heavily on rules and structure in much the same way musicians rely on the rules and structure of the orchestra. OGP is unique in that participants do not interact directly with each other, as is the case in traditional group dynamics. Like the music produced by an orchestra, participants are subliminally affected by listening to the responses of others without being distracted by verbal interaction. The group structure also provides a secure environment that is bolstered by this absence of exchange.

This illustration is merely a visual symbol of the orchestrated structure, and provides a conceptual framework for the tools and worksheets that support the

OGP. In reality, the ideal number for group participation is between 15 and 25. The semi-circle sections stop at the point where each participant can view the conductor, soloist and visual backdrop.

The original use of orchestra and "conductor" metaphor in group matrix processes came from Foulkes in the 1950's and continued in the widely written-about Tavistock tradition. The Tavistock structure has been used to help individuals focus on leadership and authority, including using a variety of group formats to help participants better understand their behaviors in groups and other organizations. Following the Tavistock tradition, group participants learn to identify specific situations that produce their most positive or negative emotional states and behavioral responses (Bion, 1961; Rice, 1969; Redlich & Astrachan, 1969). OGP is also similar in that it helps participants identify how they would react to a variety of experiences that are provided by the focus of group "soloist." The "soloist" changes with each group process and thus provides a wide spectrum of experiences, from joy to suffering, that have been identified as "pivotal" or life altering. Aspects of this technique are also similar to Kaplan and Sadock's "Structured Interactional Group Psychotherapy (1971) in which groups were structured to provide an environment for the restructuring dysfunctional schemas and behaviors.

The development of G-OM was also influenced by traditional interactional group therapy processes (Yalom, 1974), relapse prevention (Marlatt, 1985, 2002), Khantzian's model of group therapy (1990, 1992, 2001, 2004), self-psychology (Kohut, 1971), and the impact of disorders of self in relation to mood alteration and impact on self-esteem (Flores, 1997). In addition, Nobel Laureate Gerald Edelman's mind/brain theory (Edelman, 1996) helped expand the model to include how behavior constructed during extreme state conditions, which is repeated and evolves over time, becomes neurologically entrenched in the still-developing brain. The theoretical foundation of the G-OM approach has been published in a book entitled *The Orchestration of Joy and Suffering: Understanding Chronic Addiction* (Gerwe, 2001) and also translated into Russian.

The G-OM and OGP approach were developed initially within inpatient hospital-based addiction treatment setting where group therapy is a common treatment approach. OGP became an integral part of that treatment program due to the perceived improvement in the overall treatment outcomes and the information it generated further helped patient assessment and treatment planning. Over time, assessment instruments, questionnaires, tools and worksheets were developed. This treatment manual was developed to help clinicians implement the method into a variety of addiction/mental health settings.

Similar to other behavioral therapies, the primary target of OGP is *behavior*. The first statement that is posed to patients during a session is, "Have you ever said to yourself, 'Why did I do that? I am never going to do that again. Tomorrow, I will begin a new life without that behavior.' And then, before you have a chance to congratulate yourself on your success, you do the behavior again." We all have some behavior that falls into this category. The purpose of OGP is to identify the origin and path of patterns of behavior that persist in creating these problems, and to identify the feelings, physical symptoms, and perceptions that drive and maintain the behaviors. Participants have reported that they are intrigued by the first group session because it focuses on something different than is typically expected, and is conducted in a way that captivates attention.

G-OM differs from traditional cognitive behavioral therapy approaches in that it expands beyond addressing current cognitive functioning (thinking and behavior) to investigate and identify factors linked to past experience that, when triggered, produce an extreme reaction comprised of feelings, physical symptoms, perceptions, memory, and behavior components that powerfully interact and at times overwhelm the person's ability to think or act rationally when re-triggered.

OGP IMPLEMENTATION

The Orchestration Group Process can be implemented into an intensive inpatient or outpatient mental health/addiction treatment setting. It is ideally suited to an 8 to 12 week program coinciding with traditional models of addiction treatment. OGP enhances rather than competes with traditional approaches, and works well with the 12-Step Program. The group process is most effective when conducted twice a week over an extended period because it has accumulative value to those who participate. Three hours should be allotted for each session to provide enough time for group preparation, brief, introductory lectures, and group time. A third weekly session is advisable for worksheet exercises and behavioral development plans. OGP provides an important needed added dimension to treatment of PTSD and SUDs and allows ample time for other treatment processes to be conducted. An added feature is that OGP can be conducted with a small or large number of group participants.

CORE COMPONENTS OF THE ORCHESTRATION GROUP PROCESS METHOD

Key Roles in OGP:

| OGP Conductor | OGP Soloist |
|---|---|
| Feelings Row Participants | Behavioral Row Participants |
| Group Recorder | |

Key Tools in OGP (described and illustrated in Chapter 3):

| Lifespan Chart (LC) | Level of Intensity Meter |
|---|---|
| Daily Prediction Scale (DPS) | Memory Episode Dynamic (MED) |

## THE OGP "CONDUCTOR"

OGP is led by the facilitator/conductor. The conductor is responsible for the pace and flow of the process. The conductor is the guiding force, the behavioral example, and is responsible for exemplifying objectivity, compassion and investigative courage while ensuring the structure and integrity of the process. The Conductor prepares the room prior to the group therapy session by drawing the Memory Episode Dynamic on a blackboard or whiteboard backdrop. It is also a visual representation of how the group is structured and serves as a backdrop to the group conductor and soloist and should be in direct vision of the group participants. The conductor will write the identified information in the appropriate circular sections of the visual concept as it is being disclosed.

**The Soloist:** The group member chosen as soloist should be well acquainted with the OGP and should have participated in the group process prior to being chosen as a volunteer. The conductor can then better assess level of stabilization and who is most appropriate for this role. The soloist should be chosen based on his or her desire to share an experience that is regularly present in thoughts as memory. In OGP, it is never appropriate to probe for memories that the person does not have, or pressure someone to volunteer. It is not necessary for every member of group to be a soloist.

**The Feelings and Behavior Rows:** The feeling row is the ideal place for a new participant to begin once a regular group has been established. Feeling row participants are instructed to try to imagine what they might have felt if the experience shared by the soloist had happened to them. They will also be asked to describe physical symptoms that typically occur when the feelings they identify are generated. The behavior row is ideally made up of those who have participated in the feeling row, unless this is the first group for everyone. Behavior row participants are asked to try to imagine how they might have behaved if the shared experienced had happened to them.

**Group Recorder:** During each OGP group session, one group participant is assigned the role of "group recorder." This is typically a "behavior row" participant who has participated in several OGP groups. A worksheet designed for this purpose and a worksheet case example is provided at the conclusion of this chapter.

**Typical Session Flow** begins with initial focus on the soloist: Once everyone is seated and OGP guidelines and rules are explained, the conductor begins with the following questions directed to the soloist: What was your approximate age when the episode occurred?

How often does the experience you are about to share rise in your mind as memory? The most common answers to this question are: "Once a week." "Once a month." "Once a year." "Every so often." "Every single day."

Now that you have shared a brief background, can you describe what happened, the details of the episode that rise in your mind as memory?

As the soloist begins to share memory details, the conductor writes them into the vivid center circle on the blackboard. If the soloist begins to identify feelings, the conductor gently guides him/her back to the core details of the experience. The core details also include perceptions of the event and should be fully explored before beginning to identify the feelings that were generated during the experience. The conductor is patient and encouraging. The details are important because they provide clues to current feelings/symptom/behavioral triggers. It takes no more than a few minutes to fill in the central vivid detail circle. Some soloists will identify only a few recalled details and others will have many.

The conductor now asks, "Now that you've described the details that rise in your mind when you recall the experience, can you now identify what you felt during the experience? With gentle guidance and inquiry, the conductor allows the soloist to describe the feelings that were generated during the experience in his/her own words. The identified feelings are then written on the visual concept in the circle surrounding the vivid detail circle. The soloist normally identifies several feelings. Every so often, a behavior will be identified as a feeling. The conductor simply acknowledges it as a behavior and guides the soloist back to feeling identification.

When the conductor feels comfortable that the feeling response has been fully explored, focus turns to physical symptom identification with the following questions:

"When you felt the feelings you identified, can you describe what was happening in your body, your physical symptoms?" Physical symptoms are often described metaphorically. For example, "I felt hot, sweaty, and at the same time, frozen stiff, while my stomach was tied up in knots." The descriptions, however strange, may be the best way the person can explain what he or she physically experienced during the episode. The combination of feelings and physical symptoms play a crucial part in the experience and that is why they can still be recalled along with the experience. Feelings and physical symptoms represent a powerful interrelated dynamic that can develop into the most vulnerable negative emotional states of the individual and be the propelling factor in behavior repetition. These combinations are unique to each individual. At this time, the soloist is not asked to share the behavioral response, but is instead asked to wait until the group responds to what they have heard.

**Focus now turns to the group.** Beginning with the feeling row, the conductor calls upon each participant in turn to provide feedback on how each would have felt (feelings) and to identify physiological sensations or symptoms (i.e., physical reactions) he/she would likely have experienced if the situation described had happened to them. Sometimes, a new participant will identify a behavior instead of a feeling. Gently correct and ask one more time if a feeling can be identified. For example, the conductor might say, "Screaming would be more in the category of behavior, Janet. Can you identify the feeling you felt before you screamed?" Some participants feel naturally compelled to describe behavior because behavior relieves feelings and symptoms that are naturally generated when the soloist shares the experience. But identifying behavior is the job of the behavior row, and when the feeling row participants have completed their turns, the focus moves there. Behavior row participants then share how each would have behaved if the situation described had happened to them.

The behavior row participants are usually anxious to begin. The behavioral responses are as varied as the feeling row responses and revealing in relation to the behavior of each group member. Momentum and spontaneity are most evident when the behavior row is in action. The behavior row acts as closure to the group dynamic in that the atmosphere intensifies during soloist and feeling row disclosure much like the escalating dynamic that occurs during actual pivotal experience. When the behavior row disclosure begins, the intensity level begins to de-escalate much like behavior works during pivotal experience.

Momentum is created as the conductor maintains a time-oriented approach, giving each person equal time (approximately 2–3 minutes). A 1½hour time period is sufficient for a large group session. Participants often eagerly wait their turn and typically everyone participates. Spontaneous disclosure is common and consistently reflects the most immediate feeling, symptom, and behavioral reactions of participants. These responses assist participants in identifying their most predominant long-standing feeling/physical symptom combinations and most impulsive behaviors. In sequence, the conductor moves from right to the left of the feeling row, then the same with the behavior row. After participants have all had their turn, the focus once again returns to the soloist. The soloist often experiences an alteration or reframing of the experience shared after listening to the reactions of others.

The soloist is then asked to describe the behavior that was enacted in response to the experience shared. The conductor takes time to write every aspect of the behavioral response within the behavior response circle of the visual concept. The conductor gently asks investigative questions about the actions that were taken, even if the action was to stand still, such as, "How long did you stand there before moving?" "What was going on in your mind, your thought actions?" "When you finally moved, where did you go, what did you do?" When the conductor is satisfied that the behavioral response actions have been identified as thoroughly as possible, the behaviors are reviewed. The conductor then asks if the behaviors repeated and developed into patterns that have created problems. The inquiry leads to the present to determine if the behaviors are still present in the soloist's current life and to what extent they are problematic and present risk. This is invariably so unless the person has done significant work in addressing them. Once the patterns are identified, the soloist and the group are able to understand that these identified behavior patterns are a treatment issue. Group members also consider their own behavioral responses in this regard. Group concludes at this point when the process comes full circle.

**Group therapy "rules for participants":** Clinical experience has helped to recognize the need to provide some structure and rules for the group therapy session. The therapist is encouraged to encourage the participants to have no verbal interaction between group participants, or questions to the conductor or soloist during the group process. Participants sometimes have memories of their own experiences during the group process; however they are asked to refrain from sharing the experience until after group concludes. The only memory permitted for sharing during the group process is the one shared by the soloist. Otherwise, the group process and participants could easily be sidetracked by a multitude of shared memories. If someone spontaneously begins to describe a different experience, the participant should be gently guided back to the assigned role of identifying either feelings or behavior. Participants are expected to remain present until the group concludes.

## THE ORCHESTRATION GROUP PROCESS IN SESSION

The following is a case-example that illustrates the OGP technique previously described. This example is not an actual therapy session and does not include any descriptors of an actual individual treated. The case simply illustrates the concepts and clinical issues that can occur in a typical session using the OGP approach. As in all clinical treatment, clinical practice must follow all appropriate confidentiality procedures.

**Setting**: Outpatient group treatment with about 15 individuals in the group therapy session. Dr. Gerwe is the therapist of the group and serves as "the conductor." This particular session focuses on one of the patients – "Jim." Jim volunteered to be the "soloist" and the focus for this group session.

**History of the "Soloist"**: Jim is currently in treatment for alcohol dependence. He had two previous addiction treatments and a short period of sobriety before relapse and several more years of alcohol dependence. He has legal charges pending for driving while intoxicated and parole violation. His parole is related to a history of arrests for breaking and entering. He grew up in a foster home, but has two sisters who are supportive and with whom he has a close relationship. He is well mannered, exhibits a positive attitude, cooperative behavior, and expresses desire for recovery. He has been addressing current issues, alcohol dependence, pending legal charges, financial issues and unemployment. He attends the required thrice-weekly meetings of Alcoholics Anonymous (AA) and has a sponsor.

**The Group Process:** When Jim takes his chair, he has been waiting for several days to share the experience he is about to disclose. Prior to this, he has participated in G-OM for almost four weeks. During that time, while participating actively in sessions focused on other patients in the group, he identified his most distressful feelings and associated physical symptoms and his most repetitive and problematic behavior. He also identified the period in his life that he recalls first experiencing them; he was 6 years old.

As Jim sits and faces his treatment peers, I sit in a chair opposite him. There are 6 feeling row chairs semi-circled around us. There are 9 behavioral row chairs semi-circled around the feeling row. When everyone is seated, I stand and begin to conduct the process. As the conductor of OGP, I am the guiding force and the person in charge. The rules of group* are understood and accepted by all involved. Behind us, a blackboard is situated with a drawing that represents the OGP dynamic so that everyone will have a clear visual image of the pivotal experience concept. As I guide Jim through the vividly recalled memory details of his experience, I will write them in the centermost circle of three circles on the blackboard. This circle represents the vivid details that were captured in memory when the experience occurred. Surrounding this is another circle in which I will add the feelings and associated physical symptoms that he identifies in response to his experience. And then, after the group responds, one at a time with their responses, I will write in the third circle surrounding the feelings and physical symptoms, the behavior he recalls enacting in response to the experience. At this point, I will investigate further with a few more questions, and together, we will determine if the behavior/s he identified in relation to the shared experience has evolved into patterns that are problematically present in his current life, and to what degree.

I now include the reader in the process as we learn from Jim about the experience he volunteered to share. I begin by asking Jim how often the experience rises in his mind as memory. He replies that he thinks of it at least once a week, and sometimes, every day. He shares a brief background of his family and home environment at the time of the event. When he begins to describe the event, I start writing the most significant details within the center circle.

Jim begins, "I can't remember much before that day, except that we didn't have much after my Dad died. I don't remember much of him; we were not close. He went away before I was five and never returned. He was gone a lot before then, but always sent my mother money. When the money stopped coming, my mother started falling apart. I had two younger sisters by then and I tried to take her place with them, not really knowing how, but I tried. My mother didn't have any family around that I ever heard of. She went to work and my sisters and I were left alone a lot, but I don't remember trouble. We were pretty close, the three of us."

"Then, a man and woman came to the house one day and took us away when my mother was gone and we ended up in a state orphanage. It was a large stone building with two separate sections. My sisters lived in one section with girls, and I was in a section with boys. I could see them across at different times during the day, but we were not allowed to play together. Then one day, they were gone. It was horrible. But that isn't what I remember most. What I remember most—all the time—is the day my mother came there. It was morning and I was brought down to a room on the main floor. I saw my mother down the hall and ran to her. I thought she had come to take me home. She cried when she saw me and held me to her and cried even more and so did I. She told me how much she loved me and that she had been very sick and needed more time to get better. She told me that my sisters were living with a nice family but they could not take boys there. She made me promise to be a good boy and said she would come back for me as soon as she was well. She said she loved me over and over. When she had to leave, they tried to take me back to my section, but I broke away from them. I ran after her out the front door. She was in a car that was already going down the road. I ran and ran but could not catch the car. I remember the road. I can still see that road as the car got smaller and smaller—that road and the dust and the leaves falling and scattered everywhere. It must have been fall."

The room is silent. The feeling row participants are imagining themselves at age 6 and how they might have felt. I have written the vivid details in the circle on the board. They include: it was morning, the hallway, running to mother, the words spoken, the promise, mother leaving, being held back, breaking away and running after mother and out the door, the road, the dust, the leaves, the car smaller and smaller—it was fall.

I ask Jim, "Can you describe what you felt, Jim? What feelings can you identify?"

He responds, "I felt terrified, alone, abandoned, empty, an awful emptiness. I felt left behind, sad, terribly sad and lonely, lone. I felt like parts of me were gone. I felt small, getting smaller, like the car got smaller going away from me, small and alone, afraid and completely powerless."

I ask, "When these feelings became overwhelming, Jim, can you recall how you felt physically, in your body?" "Yes," he replied, "I felt weak and empty, like there was a real hole where my stomach used to be. There were other holes too, but I can't tell you exactly where. I felt sick too, weakness sick, like my legs felt weak and I ached, mostly in my chest, my heart I guess. I was crying. I remember my face felt was wet and hot."

As Jim describes his feelings and physical symptoms, I write them in the circle surrounding the vivid central details. I then ask him to turn and look at the feeling/physical symptom combination. This is a visual exercise to help Jim gain objectivity and to see what he has been feeling in external written form. I ask him if there are any other feelings or symptoms he would like to add to the circle. He replies quietly, "No."

I do not at this point investigate what Jim did (his behavior) but instead move my attention to the feeling row, and the first person (Mary) seated to the right of the semi-circle that faces us.

**The Feeling Row:** I ask, "Mary, how do you think you would have felt if this experience had happened to you at age six?" She replies, "I would have felt devastated, hurt, and unbelievably lonely and afraid." I inquire, "Mary, have you ever felt these feelings?" She replies, "Yes." Then I ask, "When you feel these feelings, Mary, how does your body respond?" Mary replies, "My stomach—I would have become nauseated and I would have been crying and not able to swallow or breathe right." I reply, "Thank you Mary."

I move from Mary to John, the person seated next to her. John identifies feelings of abandonment, anger and shame, with physical symptoms headache, tension and blurred vision. The next person, Sally, identifies, terror, guilt, desperation and despair, with symptoms she identifies as numbness in the legs and trembling in her arms with heart palpitations. As we move down the row, some share the same feelings, and two share similar symptoms, but each response is very individual and no combination of feelings and symptoms is replicated. All responses are empathetic. A few can relate to the experience, two had similar experiences, and one became tearful, but no one had trouble imagining how they might have felt.

In G-OM, it consistently occurs that when the soloist describes his or her experience and then begins identifying feelings and physical symptoms, feelings and physical symptoms are generated in the listening participants. But these are not new feelings and symptoms mysteriously triggered by listening to what the focus-of-group is sharing. They are familiar feelings that have been previously experienced, which makes it possible for the conductor to easily help each person identify them and the physical symptoms that accompany them (incredibly, many have not previously associated their physical symptoms with feelings they frequently experience). As each person shares his or her response, some respond more emotionally than others. Participants learn to trust the process having the knowledge that we will soon move to the behavior row and experience de-escalation in feeling/symptom reactions. The behavior row participants are usually eager to begin because they, too, are feeling this intensity at various levels.

By separating the feeling row from the behavior row, the group learns the difference between feelings and behavior. They learn how escalating feeling and physical symptom combinations can propel behavior at certain levels of intensity. They learn how generated feelings and physical symptoms can quickly escalate to an extreme level during certain experiences. They learn that when the combination reaches an extreme level, behavior that acts as a regulator or solution can also be a problem, for that very reason. This is exemplified when the behavior row participants share responses that are often characteristically problematic in nature while also being solution-oriented—the intensity generated by the feeling row disclosure deescalates during this sharing. The behavior we are looking to identify is not just Jim's behavior, but also the behavior that is most likely to be enacted by each behavior row participant. Jim is the catalyst that enables these revelations to occur.

**The Behavior Row:** Moving to the behavior row, I ask, "Bill, how do you think you would have behaved had this experience happened to you at age six?" He immediately replies, "I can tell you what I would have done. I would have kept running down the road and they would have had to chase me to kingdom come. Then, I'd fight and kick if they caught me and I'd have given them trouble from that day on."

I reply, "Thank you, Bill" (I can imagine little Bill doing just that because it aptly describes his present-day behavior). It consistently occurs that when participants think of themselves at a younger age, frank and honest disclosure spontaneously emerges. I move on to the next person, keeping a regulated pace, "Joe, what would you have done?" He replies, "I would have just stood there, then walked on back and went to my room and stayed to myself. I would have thought about what to do next but probably just stayed to myself and not talked about it to anyone." "Thank you Joe, "Murray, what would you have done?" Murray replies defiantly, "I would have screamed and yelled at that car and at everyone who came near me. And I can tell you, I'd have been cussing too. I would have told them all what I thought of them and her too. She shouldn't have left me. I would have told 'em all I didn't care a lick. That's what I would have done." "Thank you, Murray. Margaret, how would you have behaved?" Margaret replies sheepishly with a quavering voice, "I don't know. I think I would have just stayed there waiting for her to come back until they came to get me. And then I would have waited and waited. I think I would have prayed for God to bring her back." I inquire further, "Margaret, what would you have done if God didn't bring her back?" She replies, "I would have just kept waiting, waiting and waiting and wondering why God wasn't helping me." I move on, "Jack?" Jack replies with a nonchalant air, "I'd have said to myself, 'To hell with it,' and tried to make friends inside the joint. I'd have figured her for dead and left it at that. Oh, I'd have been upset all right, but I wouldn't let anybody know it." I reply, "Thank you Joe, and you Sharon?" Sharon replies, "I would have gone back to the place and tried to behave like I promised my mother I would and I would have been the best girl there and make my mother proud of me." (Of course, Sharon is the best-behaved person in treatment).

I continue, "And you, Tim, what would you have done?" He replies angrily, "I'd make somebody pay. At six, I guess I would have had to stay, but I'd find a way to hurt those people there in some way, maybe wreck some part of the building or something like that, probably wrecked some part of one of their cars." I ask, "Tim, why the cars?" He replies, "Well she went away in a car, didn't she?" I continue, "Would you do this openly or secretly." He replies, "They'd never know who did it if that's what you mean." "Yes, Tim, that's what I mean. So you are saying that you could devise a secret destructive plan and act it out without getting caught?" Anger gone, Tim replies with a grin, "Sure, I can."

As we continue down the behavior row, the mood lightens and it appears obvious that some are anxiously waiting their turn. The behavior that is shared is often surprising. What is most fascinating is that each person reveals behavior that seems to make absolute sense to him or her and is often surprised that other responses are not the same. Group members gain knowledge about how diverse behavioral responses can be, and how impossible it is to accurately guess what another person will do in an extreme circumstance. Although I have facilitated this process hundreds of times, I continue to be amazed at the limitless ways that human behavior is constructed during pivotal life-altering experiences.

After the last behavior row participant has shared, we all look at the blackboard, where I have written some of the feeling/symptom combinations and behavioral responses shared by the group. These visual images represent the powerful inter-related dynamics that are being individually identified. Jim has been sitting in the midst of this facing the group and listening to and observing the varied responses to his experience. The focus of my attention turns once again to him. Everyone is eager to learn what Jim did in response to the experience he shared (the behavior). I ask, "What did you do, Jim, when the car was gone from sight?"

He replied, "I ran. I ran to a nearby wooded area and hid beneath a pile of underbrush. I hid there for a long time and I heard them searching for me. Someone even came near the pile and I held my breath until he passed. I hid until dark and went over and over in my head what my mother said. I came to the conclusion that she must have been real sick but I didn't know what that meant. I thought it might mean that she had to be in a place like I was in and maybe for a long time. I thought about my sisters and I made a promise to myself to find them one day. I made a promise to myself to get stronger and bigger and smarter so I could find them. I would find my mother if she was too sick to come for me. I laid there for hours and hours and it started getting dark. I was hungry but not real hungry because of the hole inside of me. It wasn't hunger but the dark that made me go back. It was bad enough being completely alone in the daytime, but at night, I couldn't take it. I could see the lights of the orphanage off in the distance and followed them back to the road, and back to the place where I ended up staying until I was ten years old."

I stop him for a moment and ask, "Jim, the behavior you enacted was to run after your mother until the car disappeared in the distance, and then you ran into the woods and stayed hidden while you reviewed the situation over and over situation in your mind. Then you made a decision about getting stronger and a promise to yourself to find your family, followed by your return to the orphanage. What happened after you returned to the orphanage? Can you identify any other behaviors that began around this period?"

Jim replies: "I know that's when I started stealing, but it was nothing really, in the beginning. During those years, I didn't give them any problem and even liked two of the women who worked in the office section where I had chore duty. I got special favors sometimes from them and attention. I ate a lot, and tried to think strong and be strong. I did okay in their school but that wasn't the kind of smart I needed. But there was one teacher, I liked her. I needed to know how to find out about things. They wouldn't give me any information, and I quit asking. But I did start taking things from the offices when I had the chance, stealing things. I didn't know about files, but I did look through things and sometimes took papers hoping I might find out something, maybe find out about my family, and I took small things from the desk drawers, which I later threw away in the trash. There was no place safe to hide what I took. Some of the other kids got into trouble a lot, but I didn't, I didn't get caught once."

"One day, I was called into the office and met the man and woman who became my foster parents. After I went to live with them, my foster mother told me that my mother had died. She tried to comfort me but the hole inside of me seemed even larger. I did okay with them but continued stealing, both from them and breaking into places. I never took much, mostly things that weren't missed and I didn't get caught. I was fifteen the first time I got caught. I also started drinking about that time. I broke into a neighbor's house and was caught red-handed. I was sent to juvenile detention and afterward went back to live with my foster parents. But after two more arrests, I was confined for almost a year."

"A month before my release I turned eighteen. I met with a woman from social services and she started helping me. She obtained information from the state orphanage about my sisters. I learned they were living in two different places and one was in another state. Contacting them was a problem because they were under eighteen and I was told to wait. She helped me get a job at a local car factory and the job gave me some security and I did well there. But I was drinking daily after work and did some burglaries. I got involved with an older woman, moved in with her. When I had enough money, I left her and the factory and found my sisters, one by one. This was a great time in my life and I even did better for a while, got my job back and had a new girlfriend, until I got arrested again on some minor theft charge. I was always trying to help my sisters after I found them and I needed money to do this."

"Jim, your pattern of stealing seems to have initially been an effort to find out information without knowing how to get it. In other words, you didn't seem attached to the stolen goods. There was purpose in your theft, a purposeful attempt to find information or a way to your family, deal with the interim before contacting them, and then later stealing to help them. Also, there is a pattern of connecting to and receiving attention, help and comfort from women. Can you share a little more about this? You didn't mention friends at the orphanage, only the women that gave you special favors. Why did they do this, what was it about you that brought out in them that kind of attention?"

"Well, I hadn't thought about it but I guess you could say I like women, and women, for the most part, like me. It wasn't that I didn't have friends. I just didn't need friends and didn't go out of my way to have buddies. Besides, when I did things for women, they did things for me. That's why I was able to get into places in the building that the other kids couldn't, and later I got into places because I knew someone on the inside. But not my sisters, I always kept things separate from them and tried to help them whenever I could. I thought more of them than anyone."

"Jim, are you saying that women helped you in your criminal activity?" He replied, "No, I worked alone, but I always had a place to stay, someone to cover for me or vouch for me. It isn't that I use women. They all wanted to help me. The problem is they want to keep me there and I always end up leaving." I ask, "Jim, why do you leave a woman with whom you are involved? Is it that you want to be the first to leave?" "Well, maybe that was true in the beginning, but later it was usually because of another woman, or because I felt trapped. That's when the drinking gets really bad, when I'm stuck in a situation I can't get out of for a while." I ask, "Do you mean, like when you were stuck in the orphanage?" He replies, "Yeah, like then." "Jim, is there a time of the year that you are more likely to leave?" He replies after thinking for a minute, "I hadn't thought about this before but I always leave during fall. When the leaves start falling, I'm on my way. And you know what, I start drinking heavy about that time too. I hadn't put that together, but it's true. And sometimes, I take off for a while and come back to the same person. But other times, I just keep on going down the road."

"Jim, our group time is coming to a close. I have listed the behaviors you identified on the board. Your assignment is to explore in your written work how these behaviors have evolved into your present life and to determine which patterns might present risk to your recovery? We will then work together on constructing a plan of action to address the behaviors you prioritize."

The following is a list of Jim's written identified behaviors:

- Dishonesty, thievery, intrusion into private property, the property of others, lying, secrecy, strategy, planning.

- Women. Involvement in too many relationships. Taking advantage of my relationships and rationalizing my role in the relationship. Helping my sisters with money I gained illegally. They would not want this.

- Hiding. Hiding from the law, my relationships, hiding stolen goods, hiding in lots of places. Always looking for hiding places.

- No permanence. Always leaving, even when I find a nice situation. Also putting myself in not so nice situations where I get trapped for a while.

- Leaving good jobs due to law-breaking that is kept separate and secret. I do a great job and gain respect and I am loyal and honest to my employer while doing dishonest things outside my job that result in my leaving that job. I also keep my relationships separate from my job.

- I can see now how my behavior is related to certain times of the year. I start getting restless when summer ends and I have made that connection to years and years of leaving and just taking off. I've hurt people in this way and didn't even count that in. I never looked back. Well, it hurt me too.

**Summary of the Group Therapy Example:** This case exemplifies a common theme of family separation and abandonment. OGP addresses many themes and looks at the full spectrum of human experience with the primary goal of identifying experiences that produced extreme reactions and which have subsequently resulted in deeply entrenched patterns of problematic behavior linked to addiction, justification of relapse, and high risk relapse situations.

The behavior constructed by the child, when these issues are not effectively addressed, can evolve over time into behavior that becomes a driving force in that person's life. These behaviors can even appear to be positive in nature, approval seeking, and achievement-oriented in some individuals, but they are almost always obsessively driven and therefore problematic to some degree. This case provides an example of the power of pivotal experience in shaping the behavior and direction of one person's life and its influence in relation to substance abuse, dependence, and chronic relapse.

**Note:** The confidentiality of each G-OM participant is protected. Like all case example in this manual, Jim's experience is a fictional representation of an actual case and group session and just one example of the experiences shared in OGP related to family separation. Family separation and abandonment issues make up a sizable percentage of the experiences that have been shared in OGP. Whether from death, divorce, adoption, and/or repeated changes in family structure, changes in location and situations involving foster-care, hospitalizations, various levels of family dysfunction, etc., issues originating during childhood experiences that produce extreme feelings of separation, disorientation, powerlessness, loss, terror, grief, confusion, loneliness and abandonment, that are not effectively addressed or resolved, can dominate the mind, body, and spirit of a child into adulthood and be the driving force in the most problematic and obsessive behavior of the individual.

ORCHESTRATION GROUP DOCUMENTATION

Documentation is essential for recording information that is identified during the group process and transposing it into clinical notes, treatment planning, and group participant follow-up worksheets and exercises. Information accumulates with each group process as individual conditions are identified. Therefore, treatment strategies can be more individually tailored. OGP meets the recommendations of the American Society of Addiction Medicine criteria for individualizing treatment.

Page 1: Group Record of Memory Episode Dynamic on which to record the experience shared by the soloist. This document records the vivid core details of the experience, and the feelings, physical symptoms and behavior patterns identified.

Page 2 & 3: Group Recorder Worksheet designed to record each group participant's identified feelings, physical symptoms, and behavioral responses.

Gerwe Orchestration Method

## GROUP RECORDER

## MEMORY EPISODE DYNAMIC WORKSHEET

Page 1

Name _____ Today's date: _____

Age when experience occurred: _____ Birth Year: _____

Frequency of Vivid Memory: _____

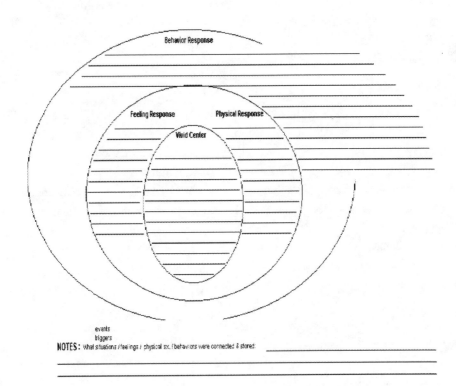

events
triggers
**NOTES:** What situations / feelings / physical sx. / behaviors were connected & stored: _____

_____

_____

Gerwe Orchestration Method

GROUP RECORDER

WORKSHEET Page 2

Date: _____ Volunteer Soloist _____ at Age____

| Name | Feeling | Physical Symptom | Behavior |
|------|---------|------------------|----------|
|      |         |                  |          |
|      |         |                  |          |
|      |         |                  |          |
|      |         |                  |          |
|      |         |                  |          |
|      |         |                  |          |
|      |         |                  |          |
|      |         |                  |          |
|      |         |                  |          |
|      |         |                  |          |
|      |         |                  |          |
|      |         |                  |          |
|      |         |                  |          |
|      |         |                  |          |
|      |         |                  |          |
|      |         |                  |          |
|      |         |                  |          |
|      |         |                  |          |
|      |         |                  |          |
|      |         |                  |          |
|      |         |                  |          |
|      |         |                  |          |
|      |         |                  |          |
|      |         |                  |          |
|      |         |                  |          |
|      |         |                  |          |
|      |         |                  |          |

| Name | Feeling | Physical Symptom | Behavior |
|---|---|---|---|
| | | | |
| | | | |
| | | | |
| | | | |
| | | | |
| | | | |
| | | | |
| | | | |
| | | | |
| | | | |
| | | | |
| | | | |
| | | | |
| | | | |
| | | | |
| | | | |
| | | | |
| | | | |
| | | | |
| | | | |
| | | | |
| | | | |
| | | | |
| | | | |
| | | | |
| | | | |
| | | | |
| | | | |
| | | | |
| | | | |
| | | | |
| | | | |
| | | | |
| | | | |
| | | | |
| | | | |

# References

Bion, W. R. (1961). *Experiences in Groups*. London: Tavistock Publications; New York: Basic Books.

Edelman, G., Tononi, G., & Sporns, O. (1996). A complexity measure for selective matching of signals by the brain. *National Academy of Science Periodical 93* (8) 3422-3427.

Feder, B., & Ronall, R. (Eds.). (2000). Beyond the hot seat: Gestalt applications to group. Montclair, NJ: Beefeeder Press.

Flores, P. (1997). Group psychotherapy with addicted populations (2nd ed.). New York: The Haworth Press, Inc.

Gerwe, C. F. (2000). *The Orchestration of Joy and Suffering: Understanding Chronic Addiction*. New York: Algora Publishing.

Kaplan, H.I. & Sadock, B.J. (1971). "Structured interactional group psychotherapy. In: H.I. Kaplan & B.J. Sadock (Eds.), *Comprehensive group psychotherapy*. Baltimore, Maryland: The Williams and Wilkins Company.

Khantzian, E.J., Halliday, K.S., Golden, S., McAuliffe, W.E. (1992). Modified group therapy for substance abusers. *The American Journal on Addictions 1*(1): 67-76.

Khantzian, E.J., Halliday, K.S., McAuliffe, W.E. (1990). *Addiction and the vulnerable* self: Modified dynamic group therapy for substance abusers. New York and London: Guilford Press, 1990.

Khantzian, E.J. (2001). Reflections on group treatments as corrective experiences for addictive vulnerability. *International Journal of Group Psychotherapy 51*, 11-20. Khantzian, E.J., Golden, S.J., McAuliffe, W.E. (2004). Group therapy. In: M. Galanter & H.D Kleber (Eds.), *Textbook of substance abuse treatment*, 391-403, (3rd ed.) Washington DC: American Psychiatric Press Inc.

Kohut, H. (1971). The Analysis of Self. New York: International University Press.

Marlatt, G.A., Parks, G.A. & Witkiewitz, K. (2002). A guideline for implementing relapse prevention therapy. A Guideline developed for the Behavioral Health Recovery Management Project. Addictive Behaviors Research Center: University of Washington.

Marlatt, G.A., & Gordon, J.R. (Eds.) (1985). *Relapse prevention*. New York, NY: Guilford Press.

Miller, W.R, & Harris, R.J. (2000). Simple scale of Gorski's warning signs for relapse. Journal of Studies on Alcohol, 6(15): 759-765.

Moreno, J.L. (1972). *Psychodrama* (4th ed.). Beacon, NY: Beacon House (Originally published in 1946).

Palmer, P. J. (1990). The active life: A spirituality of work, creativity and caring. San Francisco: Jossey-Bass Publishers.

Perls, F. (1969a). *Gestalt therapy verbatim*. Lafayette, CA: Real People Press.

Redlich, F. C. and Astrachan, B. M. (1969). Group dynamics training. *American Journal of Psychiatry*, 125, 1501-1507.

Rice, A. K. (1969) Individual, group and intergroup processes. *Human Relations*, 22, 565-584.

Yalom, I. (1974). Group psychotherapy and alcoholism. *Annals of New York Academy of Sciences*, 233, 85-103.

# CHAPTER 3. CHARTING THE LIFESPAN FROM PAST TO PRESENT

## STEP 3: THE OGP TOOLS AND WORKSHEETS

"In solving a problem of this sort, the grand thing is to be able to reason backward. That is a very useful accomplishment, and a very easy one, but people do not practice it much...Most people, if you describe a train of events to them, will tell you what the result would be. They can put those events together in their minds, and argue from them that something will come to pass. There are few people, however, who, if you told them a result, would be able to evolve from their own inner consciousness what the steps were which led up to that result. This power is what I mean when I talk of reasoning backward, or analytically."

— Arthur Conan Doyle. Sherlock Holmes to Watson, in "A Study In Scarlet."

Edelman explains; "The brain of each individual is unprecedented. Not only are prenatal patterns unpredictable from the from the recipe book of the genes, but after the moment of birth, every single sensory event and every internal thought has a physical impact on one's neuronal network. Thus, who we are is due as much to private history as to genetic destiny. Genetic instructions within the cells provide only general guidelines for finding each neuron's eventual location in the brain. Consequently, everyone's brain looks human but the precise structure is thoroughly unpredictable. You might as well try to divine what arrangement a flurry of snowflakes falling from a cloud will make on the ground. Thus every person, even an identical twin, has a network of connections within his or her brain different from that in every other brain (Levy, 1994)."

In relation to an extreme event, consider Edelman's (1995) assertion that the brain has the ability to uniquely construct a response to novel experience rather than simply react with what has previously been programmed into the brain. He explains how maps, synapses and circuitry, without a preordained plan, work through a process he calls *reentry*. He compares this process to a string quartet in which each musician is constantly processing all sorts of signals--an eye movement from one player, the force with which another applies the bow, a dip of the head from a third--that occur within an instant and enable the disparate sounds made by each to emerge into a whole. He writes, "This is the key to thought, memory and consciousness."

VIVID CORE MEMORY

G-OM case study interviewing found that memories formed during pivotal experiences that are regularly present in the current consciousness of the individual are consistently described with a **core of vivid sensory detail** representing the event. When the core details are described, it is also possible to identify the feelings and physical symptoms that were generated during the experience, the person's perception of the event, and the behavior constructed in response. The core of the memory is the window into the formula made up of **feelings-physical symptoms-perception-sensory details-behavior** that remains an inter-related dynamic with continual triggered repetition, and can be identified because of this inter-relationship.

Memories of pivotal lifespan experiences, when not regularly present, are sometimes suppressed for years until triggered by the formulated vivid center of detail stimuli. Memories of pivotal experiences can change with additional input and new information, causing speculation that memory is an unreliable foundation source for treatment. However, the vivid details captured during pivotal events remain consistently intact and are powerfully reactive to current associated stimuli. To the individual, they can seem a group of odd bits of information that might seem insignificant. A trauma episode, for example, might be described as a scenario that includes the color of the sky that day, the scent in the air, or a bird flying off in the distance. It might seem that a similar trauma event would be the primary catalyst for re-triggering, when instead, seeing a bird flying in the distance could be the main trigger, and one that is completely discounted. Identifying the key sensory elements (what is seen or heard, the scent, what is touched or tasted) during the extreme experience and captured in sensory detail provides the clues to current triggers, and is one of the most important factors in the treatment of conditions that develop from them. Recalling his childhood, Steven King writes, "Mine is a fogged-out landscape from which occasional memories appear like isolated trees . . . the kind that look as if they might like to grab and eat you."

ILLUSTRATED MEMORY IMPRESSION

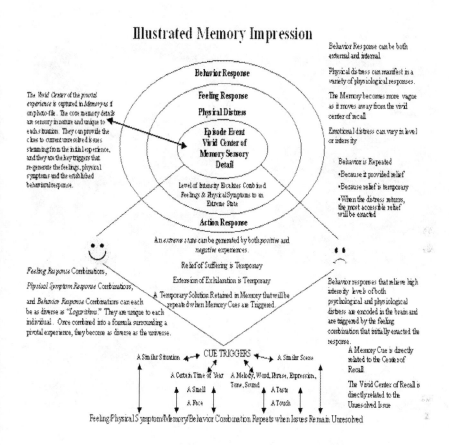

## Illustrated Memory Impression

MEMORY

   The hippocampus, named after the Greek word for seahorse (which it resembles in shape), has been shown to be critical in memory formation in relation to novel experience. Naturally, an animal could not survive if it were incapable of registering which part of the environment has already been explored or learning from experience those areas inhabited by predators. To do this the animal must first form a memory of its exploration and this task is performed by the hippocampus. If the hippocampus is destroyed, laboratory animals will return monotonously to areas of the cage where they have already visited, while seeming to ignore unexplored portions of their environment. Neurophysiological techniques, such as single cell recordings of the hippocampus, enabled psychologists to isolate novelty rather than reward as the factor that "turns on" the hippocampus to form a memory.

**The Nature and Dynamics of Pivotal Experience**

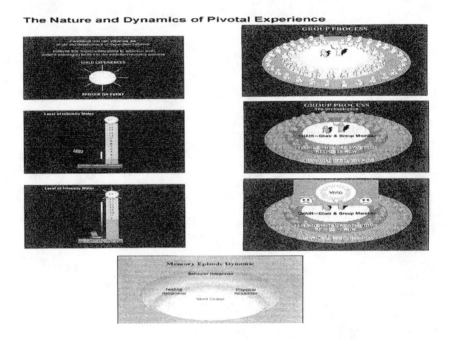

Scans that chart increased and decreased blood flows through the brain show that memories are not localized the way computer bytes are. There are some local "specialties:" different groups of nerve cells come alive to process irregular versus regular verbs, pictures of camels versus pictures of wrenches, an object's color versus an object's use. But a single memory or thought triggers many different parts of the brain simultaneously. When information about the world pours in from the senses, chemical messengers that link nerve impulses from one brain cell to another flood through the brain. As the same input is repeated, the chemical connections are reinforced: the same signals can race more quickly to their destinations and be recognized as something that all these cells have experienced before (Fischer, 2002).

Over many years, Dr. Gerwe developed a variety of tools to assist individuals in processing life-altering events that continue to disrupt current functioning. These tools provide a visual concept that reflects the nature of pivotal experiences and the core memory details that represent them. They provide a structure in which to process this information and to identify and monitor current emotional states and the events and behaviors associated with them. The G-OM uniquely blends psychodynamic and cognitive behavioral approaches to target maladaptive, addictive, and trauma related behavioral conditions and diminish the power they have to sabotage recovery processes. While the Orchestration Group Process (OGP) is the cornerstone of G-OM and provides a method to better understand the relationship of current behaviors and previous pivotal life experiences, the tools described and illustrated in this chapter work like the inter-related components of the pivotal experience they address. G-OM is a dynamic, accumulative, investigative and therapeutic approach that addresses the fundamental nature of human experience at its most extreme.

KEY TOOLS SURROUNDING OGP

**Lifespan Composition:** One of the most helpful self-investigative tools of G-OM is the **Lifespan Chart** (LC). This simple orchestrated framework helps the individual depict significant life experiences over a timeline representing personal history. The LC provides a structure to objectively explore and chart life events that have been retained in accessible memory. The LC is first assigned during the initial stage of G-OM and continues as an ongoing project. The LC is visually designed to represent the Orchestration Method, which was created to structurally represent the nature of pivotal experience as it unfolds. LC is easy-to-understand and allows each individual the freedom to creatively highlight crucial periods and life events by marking, writing, or drawing them. The result is a visual account that can be read and evaluated by the client and clinician. The LC has proven remarkably effective in facilitating a more in-depth assessment and diagnosis. The English Oxford Dictionary meaning of the word *diagnosis: to distinguish, to discern, to learn, to know, perceive,* is carried further in medicine: *the determination of the nature of a disease by careful investigation of its symptoms and history: also the opinion resulting from such investigation.*

Investigative processes are most effective when there is collaboration. Past history can seem an overwhelming minefield of information without an appropriate structure for self-investigation. G-OM was developed to provide this structure. Facilitated self-investigation helps a person to gain perspective and discover important clues relevant to current conditions.

G-OM views facilitated self-investigation that explores the link between past and present as a courageous quest for self-knowledge that makes the individual a primary player in his/her own treatment. Einstein said, "We have our own physician inside each of us."

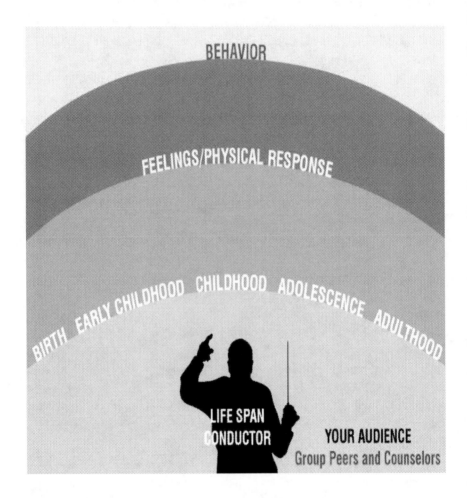

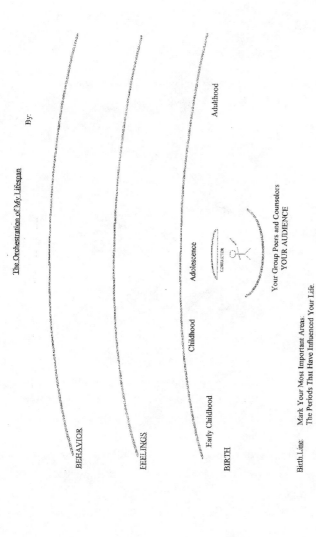

The Orchestration of My Lifespan

By:

BEHAVIOR

FEELINGS

Early Childhood    Childhood    Adolescence    Adulthood

BIRTH

Your Group Peers and Counselors
YOUR AUDIENCE

Birth Line:    Mark Your Most Important Areas.
The Periods That Have Influenced Your Life.

Feeling Line:    Write The Feelings You Most Associate
With The Lifespan Periods You Have Marked.

Behavior Line: Write The Behaviors Most Associated With The Feelings You Have Described.

86

## ORIGIN AND EVOLUTION OF THE LEVEL OF INTENSITY METER

**THE ROLE OF PIVOTAL EXPERIENCE IN PROBLEMATIC BEHAVIORAL DEVELOPMENT**

Conditions That Can Influence the Origin and Development of Dependent Patterns of Behavior

CHILD EXPERIENCES

A PIVOTAL EPISODE/EVENT

When the feeling and physical symptom response to an episode/event escalates to an extreme level of intensity beyond what the child can endure physically or emotionally.

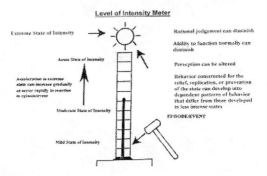

## THE DAILY PREDICTION SCALE

The Daily Prediction Scale (DPS) was developed to help G-OM participants identify daily triggers that continue to produce feeling/symptom combinations and to recognize the components that make up the most problematic conditions and responses in current life. The DPS as a daily assignment has the following benefits:

- It is a brief exercise that requires only a few minutes to complete.
- It helps the client "partialize" problem reactions to a variety of upsetting situations.
- It provides a record of progress and alerts both the client and the clinician to high-risk conditions that need attention.
- The DPS is a helpful document for the client to share during sessions with physician, psychiatrist or therapist because it reflects combinations of feelings and physical symptoms that might not present in normal circumstances, and the situations that provoke them.

- The DPS helps to reduce the level of intensity that occurs during triggering events that have previously escalated with no interference.
- It facilitates increased understanding of the propelling factors that contribute to impulsivity and obsessive preoccupation.
- The DPS is a self-measuring tool that reflects the internal/external dynamics underlying persistent patterns of behavior, increasing understanding of self and others.
- Within every 24-hour period, the DPS helps the individual segment the components of a reaction to an upsetting event into a workable approach that allows for the reality of an occasional setback.
- The DPS provides a window into the internal world of the client as he/she relates to daily life.
- The DPS provides a consistent source of data that helps to determine the course of treatment and referral.

The Daily Prediction Scale provides a structured account of daily struggles and progress. The Level of Intensity Meter on the scale works like an internalized tool for gauging reactions. The information that is documented helps to determine current level of risk in order to better assess, diagnose and implement appropriate treatment interventions and aftercare strategies.

*Daily Prediction Scale (DPS)*

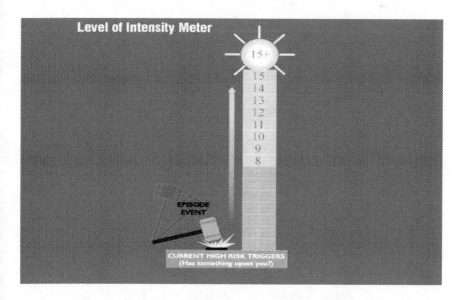

# Identifying Feelings, Physical Symptoms, and Behaviors

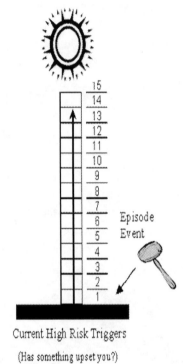

Current High Risk Triggers

(Has something upset you?)

**Describe the Event**

_____
_____
_____

**Identified Feelings**

_____
_____
_____

**Physical Symptoms**

_____
_____
_____

**Behavioral Response**

_____
_____
_____

Daily Prediction Scale

Self-Report by: _____

Name: _____

Date: _____

Level of Intensity Meter

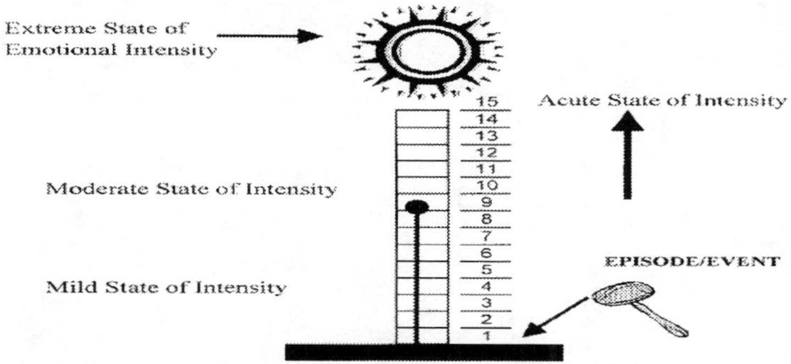

Extreme State of Emotional Intensity →

Acute State of Intensity

15
14
13
12
11
10
9
8
7
6
5
4
3
2
1

Moderate State of Intensity

Mild State of Intensity

EPISODE/EVENT

1. Current High Risk Triggers:
(Has something upset you?)

_____
_____
_____
_____
_____
_____
_____
_____

2. High Risk Feeling State:
(List current feelings)

_____
_____
_____
_____
_____
_____

3. High Risk Physical Symptoms

_____
_____
_____
_____
_____
_____
_____

4. High Risk Behavior Patterns:
Thoughts/Words/Actions

OLD
_____
_____

NEW
_____
_____

Intensity Level Range: (Within a 24 Hour Period)

1-4: _____ Hours  5-10: _____ Hours  11-15: _____ Hours  Above 15: _____ Hours

Total Hours Above 11: _____

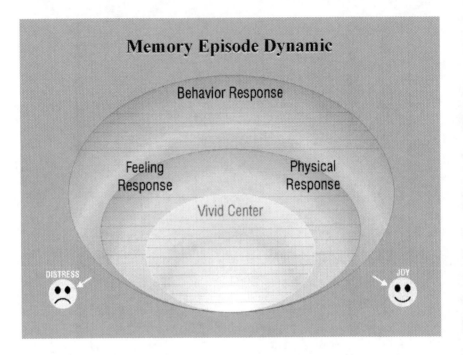

The **MED** was initially developed to address past experiences that emerge during OGP. Typically, this is not the first time the memory has occurred. It is simply that the memory has once again been stimulated into consciousness by listening to the focus-of-group's shared experience and the group participant responses. When memories occur during OGP, participants often want to spontaneously share the experience when their turn comes around. This type of disclosure is distracting when the focus should remain on the experience being shared by the soloist. Prior to each group session, it is explained that if a memory of an experience occurs during the group process, it should be considered too important to quickly describe while also doing the assigned group-row task. The memory should instead be documented on a MED worksheet at the conclusion of group, so that it can be reviewed and evaluated by the counselor and participant for further processing within the most appropriate context. The MED has several versions, is used in a variety of G-OM processes, and is a very popular worksheet that is both revealing and therapeutic.

## PRIORITIZING IDENTIFIED PIVOTAL EXPERIENCES

Once participants learn to use the Lifespan Chart (LC) and Memory Episode Dynamic (MED), they start the process of identifying their most significant lifespan experiences. Some may identify only one major experience, and others, just a few. Some identify so many experiences that they find it difficult to fit them all on the Lifespan Chart. Participants often request that the LC be made larger. This is easily done at the copy machine.

At this juncture in G-OM, participants are instructed to review their LC and begin to prioritize their charted experiences. During the Orchestration Group Process, it is impossible to focus on every experience identified on the Lifespan Chart. OGP focuses on one experience per group session so that participants learn how to understand and process experiences and apply this knowledge to each experience identified. During the G-OM process, participants identify many significant experiences. By prioritizing the charted experiences, participants learn how to address each element of the one they have chosen, and then apply what they have learned to others on the chart. It is also not necessary for each participant to be the OGP soloist because every role in OGP is equally important and insight can be gained from each. Whether sharing an experience as soloist, or listening and responding to an experience within designated group rows, knowledge of the G-OM concept and primary objectives are quickly learned and addressed in many ways and with many tools. All of these activities are preparation for life after treatment, and for addressing life events with a constructive method and in a different way that was previously known.

Gerwe Orchestration Method

## MEMORY EPISODE DYNAMIC WORKSHEET

Using the Memory Episode Dynamic below, begin writing in the *Vivid Center Circle* the details that you recall when the memory in question enters your thoughts.

In the *next circle*, write the feelings that you identify when this memory enters your thoughts.

Next, in the same circle, write the physical symptoms that came with the feelings.

In the *outer circle*, write the behaviors (thoughts, words, actions) that you can identify that occurred during and in response to this episode.

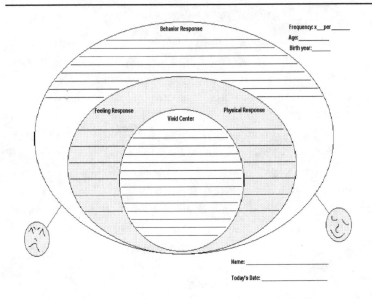

Understanding the components of pivotal experience gives participants a workable concept in which to address what may have previously been an over-whelming, disconnected, vague, and misunderstood emotional/behavioral phenomenon. Understanding the inter-related dynamic of feelings, physical symptoms, perception, memory, and behavior at its most intensified level, makes it possible to re-examine experiences that still have far too much power to disturb current functioning and potential, and to do so with more objectivity, confidence, and in full collaboration with group peers and the clinical staff. This empowers them to be able to continue to explore and address their own life experiences after discharge from a structured therapeutic/treatment environment.

## References

Edelman, G.M. (Feb. 1995). Neural Darwinism: selection and reentrant signaling in higher brain function. *Neuron*, 10 (2): 115-25. New York: Neurosciences Institute.

Fischer, J. S. (July 1, 2002). "Mysteries of Science." *U.S. News and World Report*, pp. 76-77.

King, S. (2000). *On Writing: A Memoir of the Craft*. Simon & Schuster, Inc.

Levy, S. (May 2, 1994). "Annals of Science: Dr. Edelman's Brain." *The New Yorker*.

# CHAPTER 4. MONITORING THE SYMPTOMS THAT UNDERLIE AND EMERGE

## STEP 4: "PHYSICAL MEMORY = RAPID RESPONSE" PTSD SYMPTOM IDENTIFICATION AND TREATMENT

"Things had indeed been very slow with us, and I had learned to dread such periods of inaction, for I knew by experience that my companion's brain was so abnormally active that it was dangerous to leave it without material upon which to work. For years I had gradually weaned him from that drug mania which had threatened once to check his remarkable career. Now I knew that under ordinary circumstances he no longer craved for this artificial stimulus, but I was well aware that the fiend was not dead but sleeping, and I have known that the sleep was a light one and the waking near when in periods of idleness I have seen the drawn look upon Holmes's ascetic face, and the brooding of his deep-set and inscrutable eyes. Therefore I blessed this Mr. Overton, whoever he might be, since he had come with his enigmatic message to break that dangerous calm which brought more peril to my friend than all the storms of his tempestuous life." — Arthur Conan Doyle. Dr. Watson in "The Adventure of the Missing Three-Quarter." *The Return of Sherlock Holmes*

## THE "ORCHESTRATION" OF THE HUMAN BODY

The human body is like an enormous orchestra in which the musicians perform in individual cells, all born with a sense of 24-hour rhythm. The players are grouped into various sections. Instead of strings and woodwinds, we have kidneys and livers, each composed of thousands of cellular oscillators, similar within an organ, different across organs, all keeping a 24-hour biochemical beat but entering and exiting at just the right times. Within each organ, suites of genes are active or idle at different times of day. The conductor for this symphony is the circadian pacemaker, a neural cluster of thousands of clock cells in the brain, themselves synchronized into a coherent unit (Stovatz, 2003).

Our body rhythms are the conductor of the *physical self*. We are brought into this world with the ability to endure a lot in terms of physical intensity and stress. Birth itself can be an enormously stressful event. The human child is completely dependent on the care of others in the new and wondrous environment. The tasks of learning in early childhood would seem formidable to most adults, and the dangers present are many compared to the safety of the womb. The primary role of parent/guardian is to provide a buffer and source of protection for the child. But even with protection, there is much to experience and learn that can create intense internal pressure, anxiety, and stress. We are, however, built to take it--to a certain point--and that point is unique to each individual.

In biology, there is a term "the physical takes care of itself." Our brain, for example, contains a population of oscillators with distributed natural frequencies, which pull one another into synchrony (Welsh et al. 1995). These are the cells of the circadian pacemaker, the internal chronometer that keeps us in sync with the world around us. Like the circadian pacemaker, our brain and body organs contain oscillating regulators that help maintain system homeostasis. These regulators enable us to function normally.

The limbic system in the brain is responsible for regulating emotional intensity. It occupies the lower fifth of the brain with all its parts tied bidirectionally to the hypothalamus. Brain and behavior experts have linked this interconnecting wheel arrangement to hormones, drives, temperature control, reward and punishment centers, and one part of it, to memory formation. There is a reverberating cycle by which messages can make a full circle through 5 limbic system structures: hippocampus, mammilary body, anterior thalamus, angulate cortex and hypothalamus. Simplified, the limbic system acts as the center for feeding, fighting, fleeing, and sexual behavior.

But even the best functioning systems can experience unusual circumstances that create system overload or crisis. In nature, evolutionary scientists refer to this as novel circumstance, the dictionary definition: "of a new kind or nature, strange, hitherto unknown." Novel events in nature are studied in relation to evolutionary changes in species. Novelty is now being studied in relation to defining marks of difference in neurological development and human functioning. A novel experience becomes *pivotal* when significant change occurs resulting in a unique formulization of feeling/physical symptom/perceptual/behavioral components that persist with repetition and evolve beyond the event. While we all share the highly developed brain and body similarities that make us human, individual differences within those similarities are limitless, and extraordinarily exemplified in response to pivotal experience. Poet Wallace Stevens beautifully captures this idea in "Esthetique du Mal."

> And out of what one sees and hears and out
> Of what one feels, who could have thought to make
> So many selves, so many sensuous worlds,
> As if the air, the mid-day air, was swarming
> With the metaphysical changes that occur . . .

While our brains work for us in such individual and marvelous complexity, our bodies are yet another example of extraordinary variations. The works of the great physician Galen (c. 129-c. 200 AD) were treated as the final word in anatomy for hundreds of years, despite what we now recognize as serious, even preposterous errors. It was not until 1543 that the Belgian anatomist Andreas Vesalius (1514-1564) challenged the great Galen by publishing a more accurate anatomy text based on his own observations from the dissection of cadavers. Today's technological advancements make it possible to view the human body and brain in ways that would have astounded Vesalius. And yet, those who work directly with the human body can tell stories that even the best photo-imaging scanners cannot reveal.

Dr. Sherwin B. Nuland, clinical professor at Yale School of Medicine, attests: "No matter how often a surgeon performs the same operation, it is different each time. Any operating room nurse can tell you that. The sequential precision steps so exactingly depicted in manuals of surgical technique resembles the real thing about as much as a diagram of human anatomy looks like a human being. To take something simple: Of the many hundreds of appendectomies I have done during a career of thirty-five years, no two were the same. Even such straightforward operative procedure for a straightforward disease, divisible into a short series of straightforward technical maneuvers that were standardized almost one hundred years ago, done by an operator of long experience—even under such circumstances every case is a novelty. And some of those novelties can be daunting tests of skill and confidence...Although the configurations of human innards do not vary nearly as much as do those of our outards (a word that exists in no dictionary, but should), they nevertheless reveal unmistakable variations among individuals—and only surgeons ever find out about them (Nuland, 2000)."

Nulen's description of surgical observations and findings help us to understand how uniquely individual the physical response to pivotal experience can be. G-OM development provided a method, and OGP a group context, in which participants described the feelings that were generated during their identified pivotal experiences, the physical reactions that were felt in the body during those experiences, and the effect each had upon the other. Feelings and physical symptoms were consistently identified as separate entities with unlimited variations, that when combined during the experience into the formulated response, represented the driving elements of the most problematic behavior of those participating and the behavior most resistant to change.

## PHYSICAL SYMPTOM EVOLUTION AND LONGEVITY

The impact of feeling/physical symptom combinations on the current lives of G-OM participants revealed a consistent impact on daily mood, thoughts, behavior, and current health problems and medical conditions. When the feelings, physical symptoms and associated behavior combinations were identified linking past pivotal experiences to current life functioning, their evolutionary path and longevity could be tracked and their impact on daily life measured. In many cases, the daily impact was astounding.

During G-OM development, the physical symptom component was recognized as a predominant factor in propelling the feelings and perceptual response to an extreme level during the initial pivotal experience and propelling it to an extreme level when re-triggered in current life. When it became evident that a large percentage of G-OM participants previously had not made the connection between their feelings, physical symptoms, perceptions, and behavioral actions, helping them to make these connections became an integral part of G-OM and is greatly instrumental in its effectiveness. "It is a wonderful feeling," said Einstein, "to recognize the unity of a complex of phenomena that to direct observation appear to be quite separate things."

The combination of *feelings +physical symptoms +perception* that occurs during a *beyond-the-norm* state is as unique to each person as the experiences that generate them. When these inter-related components continue to trigger an "ungovernable" state that is only regulated by the behavior constructed during the initial occurrence, it is understandable how dependence upon the behavior develops. The very term *ungovernable* suggests an inability to regulate or restrain oneself. To better understand how powerful this dynamic can be, it is necessary to understand more about one of the most driving phenomena that takes place in the human body. The physical symptom response is referred to in biological terms as "the *physical self.*"

## PHYSICAL MEMORY = RAPID RESPONSE

The physical symptom response is one of the most underestimated and consistent factors identified in relation to extreme events and can produce post-traumatic stress symptoms in varying degrees and levels of severity, whether the event or series of events happened in childhood, adolescence, or adulthood. When extreme experiences are compounded, the level of severity can increase significantly to create ungovernable states and reactions that overwhelm the person's ability to self-regulate. At the most extreme level, a point of transformation takes place that dramatically affects cognition. As in mathematics, at this point the components generated (feelings/symptoms/perception) merge together to become more than the sum of its parts and a different entity entirely. Like a percolating coffee pot that reaches a certain temperature, transforming water and grounds into coffee, the converging components are transformed at the peak level of intensity. At this level of extremity, physical symptoms can dominate cognitive functioning. The physical sensory information is captured at this point and recorded within cognitive memory and is primarily dictated by what the person touches, sees, hears, smells, and tastes (the physical) rather than rational thought. The vivid sensory details are in a sense transformed into physical memory. Recalled memories of extreme events are always described with vivid sensory details, while the surrounding experience can be limited, vague, distorted, and fragmented. The physical sense memory henceforth can become the propelling dynamic when another extreme state is re-triggered by current stimuli.

DAILY PREDICTION SCALE: Current High Risk Evaluation Alert

Self-Report by:

Name: _____

Date: _____

Level of Intensity Meter

Extreme State of Emotional Intensity

15+ Extreme State      [Physical Response Peaks]

15   Acute State of Intensity    [Physical Response *Accelerates*]

| Level | | Description | Physical Response |
|---|---|---|---|
| 14 | 14 | | [Increasing Physical Response] |
| 13 | 13 | High State of Intensity | [Increasing Physical Response] |
| 12 | 12 | | [Physical Response] |
| 11 | 11 | | [Physical Response] |
| 10 | 10 | | [Detectable Physical Response] |
| 9 | 9 | | |
| 8 | 8 | | |
| 7 | 7 | Moderate State of Intensity | |
| 6 | 6 | | |
| 5 | 5 | | |
| 4 | 4 | Mild State of Intensity | |
| 3 | 3 | | |
| 2 | 2 | | |
| 1 | 1 | | |

Episode/
Event

1. Current High Risk Triggers: _____

2. High Risk Feeling State: _____

3. High Risk Physical Symptoms: _____

4. High Risk Thoughts: _____

4. High Risk Behavioral Response: _____

Record the number of hours at each **Intensity Level Range** within 24 hours of the Trigger Event:

Above Level 15: ___ hrs.   Levels 11 - 15: ___ hrs.   Levels 5 - 10: ___ hrs.   Levels 1 - 4: ___ hrs.   Total Hours above Level 11: ___ hours.

## G-OM EXAMPLES OF IDENTIFIED FEELING RESPONSES

Rigorous documentation of feeling and physical symptom responses resulted in the following lists of identified feelings and symptoms. Below are only a few examples. In G-OM, both positive and negative experiences are addressed. Each extreme of the spectrum is given equal weight because the extreme of both joy and suffering can produce problematic patterns of behavior when not effectively addressed or resolved.

| Lonely | Sad | Hopeless | Ecstatic |
|---|---|---|---|
| Confused | Sorry | Overwhelmed | Euphoric |
| Disoriented | Stupid | Overpowered | Invincible |
| Angry | Humiliated | Ashamed | Blissful |
| Hurt | Embarrassed | Overcome | Enamored |
| Terrified | Deflated | Shame | Excited |
| Petrified | Ruined | Guilty | Joyful |
| Shocked | Desperate | Tricked | Love |
| Stunned | Deprived | Devastated | Loved |
| Surprised | Outcast | Worried | Awestruck |
| Startled | Different | Alone | Wonder |
| Afraid | Degraded | Lonely | Curious |
| Furious | Inadequate | Separate | Special |
| Mad | Insecure | Abandoned | Powerful |
| Outraged | Empty | Intimidated | Important |
| Rage | Self-conscious | Disbelief | Amazed |
| Hate | Cornered | Shunned | Enchanted |
| Desperate | Ugly | Confined | Mesmerized |
| Trapped | Invisible | Isolated | Desired |
| Suffocated | Worthless | Constricted | Protected |
| Powerless | Discounted | Alienated | Acknowledged |
| Helpless | Exposed | Frantic | Accepted |
| Jealous | Bad | Bewildered | Wanted |
| Fat | Irritated | Apprehensive | Included |
| Loathing | Impatient | Disgusted | Exhilarated |
| Irate | Rejected | Dismayed | Thrilled |
| Deceived | Dismissed | Deceived | Anticipation |
| Humiliated | Horrified | Screwed | Appreciated |
| Betrayed | Frustrated | Out-of-control | Vindicated |
| Distraught | Vulnerable | Threatened | Applauded |
| Endangered | Loathing | Lost | Mystified |
| Wary | Irate | Incredulous | Glorified |

## G-OM EXAMPLES OF IDENTIFIED PHYSICAL SYMPTOMS

loss of body fluids: tears-crying-urination-diarrhea-perspiration-vomiting

nausea — sick to stomach — burpy

rapid pulse-adrenaline rush

weakness — fatigue — lightheaded — sinking — faint — dizzy — ears ringing — weightlessness

heaviness — weighted — stone — hardened — encased — immobilized

lifeless — exhaustion — drained

raised body temperature

lowered body temperature

fluctuating body temperature

shaking — trembling — twitching — jerking

headache — migraine — burning in head — head spinning — deafness — noise in eardrums

muscle ache — soreness

tingling — electric — numbness — itching — goosebumps

blinded — vision blurred — vision dimmed — vision distorted

rapid heart beat — heart racing — heart palpitating — heart pounding

heartbroken — heartache

heart shattered

shot in the heart

heart torn apart

heart ripped apart

heart throbbing

heart in throat — heart dropped — heart sunk — heart punctured

heart about to burst — about to explode — about to stop — stopped

throat constricted — throat dry — mouth dry

inability to swallow — lump in throat — throat closed — metallic taste

difficulty breathing — shortness of breath — quick breathing — gasping — choking — gagging

knot in stomach — hole in stomach — twisted stomach — stomach ache

punched in stomach — kicked in stomach — butterflies in stomach

icy cold — clammy — cool — freezing — skin paleness

burning hot — boiling hot — blood rushing — red face — flushed face, flushed neck, chest — ears

red patches — rash — blotches — hives

head exploding — headache — tension in head, neck, arms, all over

frozen stiff (not cold) — frozen in place

energized — adrenaline — strong — activated — restless — nervousness

panic — anxiety

**Note:** *Physical symptoms* are typically described metaphorically by G-OM participants because this terminology is the best way for them to explain what is physically experienced during their most distressful/excitable states. These are only a few examples. A combination of several feelings and physical symptoms can occur to generate an extreme state. Although the list numbers in the hundreds, the eight most common *feelings* identified were anger, fear, frustration, humiliation, sadness, guilt, loneliness and shame. To give an example of just how diverse one of these feelings can be, consider *feeling row* responses given by participants in relation to the feeling *fear*. When asked to further define the feeling when identified, participants described fear in a multitude of individualized variations, for example: fear of loss, fear of abandonment, fear of death, fear of the dark, fear of punishment, fear of the unknown, fear of confinement, fear of disapproval, fear of being alone, fear of people, fear of certain places, open spaces, closed doors, water, heights, fear of objects, and countless other variations.

**The Daily Prediction Scale** is probably the most all-around useful clinical tool of the G-OM and it is applied here to monitor daily symptoms and responses. It is brief and to the point. Clients identify and describe events within each day that trigger feelings and physical symptoms. They rate the intensity and duration of their experience and briefly describe their behavioral response. Daily entries on the DPS facilitate the following:

• Daily practice discriminating low- and high-risk dynamics of the client's experience, and linking behavior to feeling states.

• A thoughtful feeling/symptom/behavioral review while completing the DPS that motivates clients to experiment with accountability for new and old behavior.

• Clients establish a self-monitoring ritual.

• The repetitive nature of utilizing the DPS helps to establish new behaviors.

- A journal of progress during treatment that helps clients and therapist identify triggers to repetitive feeling/symptom ❑ behavior patterns and record measureable progress.
- A series of completed DPS forms presents snapshots of the clients' current life and can be used to explore immediate issues and stresses, and identify risk.
- DPS responses aid documentation in clinical progress notes and progress toward treatment goals.
- The **Daily Prediction Scale** is a clinical self-report tool that helps shape positive behavior, identifies external and internal triggers for high-risk behavior, and provides valuable data for clinical documentation. The DPS is a critical component of the G-OM used to treat PTSD symptoms and SUDs, but it can also be utilized as a stand-alone clinical tool for examining mental health, addiction, and other behavior disorders.

G-OM uniquely blends cognitive behavioral therapy and psychodynamic approaches to target ungovernable states and the maladaptive, addictive, and trauma-related behaviors that arise from them. G-OM encompasses a variety of tools to assist individuals in identifying and monitoring emotional states that can fluctuate and emerge powerfully when triggered. The clues to these triggers can be found in the experiences in which they originated. During the early development of G-OM, it became evident that group structure, and visual concepts that reflect the nature and impact of pivotal experience, with each consistent identifiable component separated into workable sections, could help participants address difficult experiences in a safe collective environment. The group structure helps participants to reframe, reconstruct, and more effectively process what previously may have seemed too formidable. G-OM, in a sense, attempts to put order into the chaotic realm of the ungovernable with an analytic process that is easy to understand.

The impact of extreme novel experience that resulted in pivotal life-altering changes was the focal point of Gerwe's early investigations, beginning in the 1980's with a VA population of patients suffering PTSD symptoms and chronic addiction. The work centered on the most significant lifespan experiences of these individuals. The purpose of this course of action was to question why some returning veterans of war moved forward in recovery from addiction and war-related mental and physical injury and others became chronic in their conditions. The initial research centered on whether or not pre-existing symptoms and behaviors, stemming from experiences pre-dating addiction, are a factor in chronic addiction and co-occurring disorders. The study continued over two decades within addiction treatment populations, including military and criminal justice populations suffering addiction. The research resulted in more than 1,500 accumulated case studies based on investigative interviewing techniques developed for individual sessions, assessment questionnaires, self-report worksheets, and the highly structured OGP, all designed to elicit information regarding the most significant life experiences of each individual in order to discover whether or not common elements could be identified and treated. The result is the G-OM.

G-OM is considered to be an innovative approach to the simultaneous treatment of PTSD and addictions. The military, both Army and Navy, have shown great interest in its application to assess and treat returning combat veterans. There is currently a G-OM research project underway to test its efficacy within a VA setting and population.

Recent estimates of the prevalence of behavioral health problems among troops returning from active duty suggest high rates of PTSD and substance use disorders. Among the priorities identified by the National Research Council report are a better understanding of emotional reactions to stressful situations and the effects these emotions have on long-term health and functioning. Most current approaches to PTSD have been found lacking in the documentation of superior results, just as the varied approaches to the treatment of substance use disorders have not demonstrated generally superior results with any given treatment model. Most treatments for PTSD do not address the true underlying neurological dynamics that result in emotional distress and maladaptive behaviors. G-OM, developed over the course of more than 25 years in treating chronic VA recidivists and PTSD sufferers, addresses both PTSD and addictive disorders by dealing with the underlying neurological dynamics responsible for continued emotional distress and maladaptive behavior patterns.

Current studies conclude that most primary treatments for PTSD need further study for effectiveness. The International Society for Traumatic Stress Studies (ISTSS) issued new PTSD practice guidelines using a grading system. The Guidelines label several treatments in the "A" category based on their apparent degree of empirical support. These treatment models include: prolonged exposure therapy, cognitive processing therapy, stress inoculation training, other forms of cognitive therapy, eye-movement desensitization and reprocessing (EMDR), and medications. In October 2007, the Institute of Medicine (IoM), at the request of the Department of Veterans Affairs, issued a report that concludes that there is still not enough evidence to say which PTSD treatments are effective. The IoM panel concluded that few therapies have enough evidence to recommend them as treatment models to be promoted.

In a review of 53 drug studies and 37 psychotherapy studies, the seven-member panel concluded that many PTSD studies are flawed in terms of design and high drop-out rates, which limit their generalizability. The report finds most drug studies were funded by pharmaceutical companies, and many psychotherapy studies were conducted by people who developed the techniques or by their close collaborations. In conclusion, the report suggests that Congress should provide resources to the VA and other federal agencies to fund high-quality PTSD research that includes veterans and other affected groups.

The situation is similar for the treatment of substance use disorders. A recent meta-analysis of addiction treatment studies found that no treatment model has demonstrated consistent statistically significant superior results to other methods. Among those differences documented, a substantial proportion of the differentials appeared to be related to researcher allegiance to a given model – that is, researcher bias.

The US Army Research Institute for Behavioral and Social Sciences charged the National Research Council with examining current PTSD research and developing a long-term research agenda. A panel of social and behavioral science experts concluded that Department of Defense funding support six main areas of research. Two of these areas are the study of emotions and behavioral neuropsychology. These two categories are addressed by the Gerwe Orchestration Method (G-OM).

The propelling impetus was the growing evidence from these cases that certain consistent factors were identifiable and could be found in the case-by-case descriptions of the most extreme states each person experienced. Unlike most psychological tests that use a normative approach using the same scales to describe all clients with scores interpreted from a set of norms, the idiographic G-OM interviewing and case study approach revealed a different set of variables used to describe each person, while also recognizing the identified consistencies of inter-related affective, physiological, perceptual, and behavioral phenomenon constructed during experiences that generate the most extreme states for each individual. Normative techniques may be more readily interpreted in terms of individual differences, but they may not be as relevant or as penetrating as idiographic methods, which have been designed to measure variations in individuality.

The phenomenon of previous pivotal life experiences that persisted and continued to evolve over time, had significant impact on current life functioning. They also appeared to be a factor in the individual's ability to withstand and recover from the impact of current extreme events, producing a compounded effect that reduced the person's resilience to life stresses. These observations have found support in recent neurological and brain chemistry studies documenting structural and functional changes in the brain that occur in conjunction with exposure to substances and/or events. These can result in sensitivity to cues that the individual may not recognize at a cognitive level and reactions that may appear to be unrelated to the circumstance or that seem out of proportion to the precipitating event.

Given that both PTSD and addictive disorders are prevalent among troops returning from active duty, a systematic evaluation of the G-OM with this population is the logical step in determining whether this innovative approach to the treatment of PTSD and addictions may produce superior results than many of the more widely explored and promoted models. G-OM model possesses many features that meet the needs of this population, and it is well suited to a military setting because of its uniquely structured approach. Soldiers returning from deployment to combat areas overseas are at increased risk for substance abuse, addiction onset, and other high risk behaviors. Many soldiers with no prior history of problematic substance use engage in drug use or escalate their alcohol consumption upon their return.

Utilization of the G-OM ABH and/or DPS with returning soldiers holds great potential. Currently, returning soldiers receive minimal preparation regarding the potential pitfalls of reintegration with the family and guidelines for successfully negotiating this transition. At commanders' discretion they may also receive talks related to the risks of substance abuse, STD's, anger management techniques, solving and avoiding financial problems, and available support services. However, there is no data to support that these measures actually prevent substance abuse or other problematic behaviors. Analogously, studies have shown that Critical Incident Stress Debriefing for civilian emergency personnel actually does more harm than good.

Screening returning soldiers for addiction and behavioral disorder potential presents several significant challenges. Screening tools for substance abuse are based upon recent use behavior. Returning soldiers have either had very limited access to alcohol and drugs, or they would never admit their use while deployed due to adverse consequences. The ABH and DPS answer these challenges—they assess for negative emotional state and the physical-emotional-behavioral combinations that underlie substance abuse/dependence/relapse and reflect persistent PTSD symptoms. They do so without requiring the soldier to admit to any wrongdoing. The same high-risk combinations also underlie other destructive behaviors such as domestic violence. ABH and DPS assess with a brevity that could potentially be applied to high numbers of soldiers.

The EPICON report following five domestic violence fatalities at Ft. Bragg in June-July 2002 found no individual factors other than marital discord that linked the cases. Substance abuse was not a factor in any of the deaths. It further concluded that the fear of adverse career consequences significantly inhibits utilization of prevention and treatment services available in the army. However, the ABH or the DPS could be administered to an entire company anonymously. The data regarding negative emotional state, level of intensity, and risk associated with thought-behavior combinations in the past could be presented to the unit commander for further preventive actions. The G-OM could even be conducted with entire units because it is not pathology based. It is founded on the premise that normal and ethical people develop both healthy and problematic behavior patterns under intense conditions. G-OM could be taught to military mental health paraprofessionals and could be applied by them under the supervision of behavioral health officers either in the field or upon return to the USA. Even a couple G-OM sessions would serve to demystify and de-stigmatize treatment, thus making self-referrals more likely. Data gathered from the sessions would also aid decisions regarding mandatory referral of soldiers if needed.

Apart from deployment issues, the G-OM and its associated assessment tools, the Assessment of Behavioral Health and the Daily Prediction Scale lend themselves to use in the overall army treatment and prevention setting. The Army Substance Abuse Program is prevention focused combined with brief treatment. Many soldiers enter the army with pre-existing substance abuse histories. Alcohol use frequently escalates after entry into the army, and under stressful conditions, drug abuse also increases despite the severe consequences. Soldiers are bombarded with safety briefings about the hazards of substance abuse and are urged to contact their chain of command rather than risk driving while intoxicated. Commanders make public examples of those who are caught in violation of army substance use regulations. The most frequent cause of accidental death is alcohol related auto fatalities. Despite all these incentives and disincentives, alcohol and drug abuse continues. G-OM helps explain this because the problematic behaviors based upon pivotal experience are not subject to reason.

Army substance abuse treatment is brief, done mostly in a group format, and is predominantly psycho-educational and cognitive-behavioral in format. Preliminary data from research on the G-OM model indicates that it will help set up a collaborative approach to treatment that counters the authoritarian military culture and results in much greater productive disclosure in a shorter period of time. And this can be accomplished in a structured group format. Because the treatment population is mostly in the 18-25 age range, successfully identifying and treating the underlying causes of addiction onset and relapse has the potential to prevent the progression of the disease. Recently, army treatment programs have been adding intensive outpatient programs to cope with increased severity of substance abuse and decreasing availability and funding for residential treatment. The G-OM was developed in and ideally suited for intensive outpatient programs.

CONCLUSIONS

None of the current approaches to the treatment of PTSD and/or substance use disorders shows superior outcomes to all other therapies. Moreover, there is a lack of evidence as to how one might identify whether some individuals might be more receptive to one treatment model as opposed to another. The same may be said for the treatment of substance dependence. In point of fact, these two conditions often present as co-occurring conditions such that each impedes successful recovery from the other. The G-OM is a unique approach to address common elements of both PTSD and addictions. However, due to the fact that this treatment model has evolved as the life work of a single individual, it has not been subjected to rigorous evaluation by the mainstream research community. This treatment model is compatible with a wealth of current neurological research and incorporation of the method in various settings suggests that it has potential as a treatment model.

## References

Nuland, S.B. (2000). *The Mysteries Within: A Surgeon Reflects on Medical Myths.* pp. 23-24. New York: Simon & Schuster.

Rosenkranz, Z. (2003). *Einstein Scrapbook.* Johns Hopkins Press.

Stovatz, S. (2003). *SYNC: The Emerging Science of Spontaneous Order.* New York: Theia.

Welsh D.K, Logothetis, D.E., Mesiter, M., Reppert, S.M. (1995). "Individual neurons dissociated from rat suprachiasmatic nucleus express independently phased circadian firing rhythms." *Neuron* 14, pp. 697-706.

# CHAPTER 5. TREATING THE BEHAVIOR TO DIMINISH ITS POWER

## STEP 5: G-OM ALTERNATIVE BEHAVIORAL PLANNING

> "A conversation ensued, which led to high words, and almost to blows, for my father was a man of a very violent temper. Seeing that his passion was becoming ungovernable, I left him and returned towards Hetherly Farm." — Arthur Conan Doyle: Mr. James McCarthy's testimony in *The Boscombe Valley Mystery*

At this point in the G-OM process, the investigation and identification phases have reached the behavioral-action planning phase. Problematic behavior that originated during pivotal experiences evolved because it became essential to the person. G-OM creates a workshop group environment that fosters a collective teamwork approach that inspires motivation and collaboration. Participants become engaged in the process because they are learning a different way of thinking about their past experiences and the associated behaviors. Self-blame and mistaken beliefs about self and others are replaced with curiosity, insight, and increased self-awareness.

When participants learn more about the nature of behavior originating in pivotal experience, they also learn that new behavior can be constructed out of powerful new experiences. They are encouraged to develop and practice positive alternative behaviors that have the potential to overtake the deeply entrenched patterns that have previously and stubbornly resisted change. A new perspective can bring with it a new investment in self and in life. This must be fostered with behavioral work that can show some immediate results.

**Effective Intervention:** The nature of patterns of behavior born of pivotal experience must be understood if effectively treated. Pivotal experiences, when they occur, are not always observed by others or recognized for what they are. Distinct changes in behavior are a primary indication that a pivotal experience occurred. Behavior that is enacted in private or in secrecy can remain hidden for years until the behavior evolves to a point where it becomes impossible to hide. Effective intervention at the time of the experience or at an early stage of behavior repetition can stop or deter pattern development. Patterns are more likely to develop when intervention does not occur. The repeated behavioral action is only a temporary solution for re-occurring emotional states that continue to be re-triggered. The temporary nature of the resolution is the primary basis for obsessive preoccupation that can develop along with the pattern. The initial experience can remain unresolved for years while the associated patterns of behavior grow stronger and more deeply entrenched.

**Internal and External Behavior:** Pivotal experiences can produce both internal and external behavior. **Internal actions:** Perception/cognitive thoughts internally expressed and repeated (fantasizing, self-recrimination, plotting, planning, strategizing, detaching, etc.) are not observable and can consume an extraordinary amount of time and energy when obsessive preoccupation develops. **External behaviors,** like verbal or physical aggression are more noticeable. Less noticeable, are the secretive behaviors (self-abuse, eating disorders, lying, thievery, spying, hording, and a multitude of others) that can develop significantly before attracting attention. Some external behaviors can be camouflaged in positive-appearing actions such as people pleasing and attention seeking actions that appear harmless and often bring about reward but are driven by an obsessive need. In these cases, disapproval can have a devastating result, for example, compliance, placating, accommodating, pleasing, acting, humor, seduction, achievement, working toward an idealized body image, etc. When a child finds security, approval, attention, love, or relief of suffering only through these actions, dependence on the behavior is inevitable.

**The High Risk Dynamic** above illustrates how the initial response to an event can develop into high risk patterns over time. Participants need guidance and encouragement to begin developing behavioral action plans that have the power to defeat long-standing patterns that are controlling their lives. Each identified behavior pattern needs to be fully explored in order to understand the nature of the behavior, and to discover within it the natural skills and abilities of the person. New positive actions that involve the person's natural instincts, inclinations, skills, and abilities are those most likely to be practiced on a daily basis. These are the new actions most likely to work when an extreme state is triggered. New alternative actions are, in a sense, in competition with the established relied upon behavior that is being replaced. The old behavior is more powerful in the beginning stages of behavioral development and must be met with belief that it can be conquered. G-OM behavioral action plan worksheets aid in positive behavioral development, but it is equally beneficial to develop them within a supportive collective environment. The role of the clinician here is to act as a guide to positive alternative behavioral choices that have potential to take hold.

G-OM Examples of Behaviors That Were Identified as Originating In Pivotal Experience with Pattern Development Existing Prior to Addiction Onset

Isolating, withdrawal, avoidance, seclusion

Acting, pretending, hiding feelings

Secret-keeping at own expense, to protect others, to avoid shame, to avoid trouble, to avoid punishment

Lying: to protect, to deceive, to trick, to cover-up for self or another, to manipulate, to create a crisis, to get attention, approval, someone in trouble, someone out of trouble, for reward, for gain.

Dishonesty: stealing, cheating, blaming others for own wrongdoing, deceiving others and self, denial of responsibility for actions or wrong-doings

Verbal aggression: screaming, shouting, arguing, cursing, questioning, demanding, verbal self-abuse, verbal abuse towards other, tantrums that include self-abuse actions and/or self-hyperventilation.

Retaliation: covert or overt

Pleading, apologizing when not wrong or guilty, begging, complying, agreeing despite believing otherwise, negotiating, bargaining to protect self or others

Self-abuse: hitting, punching, scratching, digging, cutting, inserting objects, ingesting substances, biting, sticking pins/needles, pulling out hair, banging head, etc.

Fantasizing about death, revenge, escape, retaliation, power, being another person, being in a different place, with different people, being in different circumstances, being a super-hero

Self-recrimination, self-blame, punishing self with internal thoughts and/or verbal expression

Self-depreciation when with others, humiliating self, humor at own expense— often to deflect teasing

Pleasing others at own expense: inability to say "No"

Manipulating others in an effort to control, to dominate

Agitating others to gain attention, to provoke anger, negative response from others, punishment that cannot be self-inflicted, to engage in physical violence.

Hiding, in specific places, creating safe places, multiple hiding places

Running away, running from, escaping, eluding, deflecting attention

Disguising self, making self invisible, smaller, different in appearance

Controlling, bullying, intimidating, threatening others

High risk, life endangering actions: climbing to or jumping from high places, entering dangerous or forbidden territories, actions involving speed, chase, racing, actions involving weapons, explosives, etc.

Daring others and daring self to takes risks

Destruction of objects, places, personal belongings or the personal belongings and property of others

Fire-starting, destruction with fire-starting

Experimenting with explosives, destruction with explosives

Collecting weapons, hiding weapons, storing weapons, hoarding weapons

Collecting objects belonging to others, collecting objects for arousal, collecting objects for security

Stealing, hiding or wearing the clothing of another, wearing the clothing of another gender

Violent aggression: fighting, threatening, using weapons or a weapon of choice to aid in aggression

Hurting, killing or torturing animals

Planning and plotting retaliation/ revenge strategies

Ritualistic behavior

Sexual experimentation

Sexual imposition

Hoarding/stockpiling

Eating in secret, hoarding food

Food deprivation, self-starvation

Binge eating, then purging

Hurting self to produce an accident, to produce illness, to create sympathy, to gain attention

Creating an accident to appear heroic, to punish someone or others, to create a crisis

Watching/observing others from a hidden place, spying, peeping

Intrusive exploration into the belongings or property of others

Self-decoration that involves self-mutilation

Gambling

Impersonating another or others

Use of poisonous substances to produce illness in self or others

Deflecting attention with body language by being very still, quiet

Achievement to win security, love

Clowning: using humor to break tension, gain attention

Mediating: getting involved in disputes between others at own expense

Camouflaging self within a social environment or to hide from others

When a child experiences an extreme state that results in newly formed *constructed behavior*, the formulated connecting synapses become implanted within the neuronal structure of the still-developing brain. These behaviors are planted like a seed in nature. The synaptic seed holds within it the intricate *combination* that was formulated during the extreme state experience. Behavior repetition acts like water feeding the seed, promoting growth. Over time, the seedling develops into a firmly entrenched neuronal pathway root system with a stem-like outgrowth of limbs and branches. Stem and branch growth is fueled by repetition as the child develops increased behavioral skills and abilities that foster variations and innovations as the pattern evolves in strength, scope and dimension.

Neuronal pathway development is at peak during childhood; never again will the brain develop at such a rate. At around age 10, the brain begins to ruthlessly destroy its weakest synapses leaving only the strongest developed pathways. There are many variations within the pathway/pattern structure. Some behavior is enacted continually without any period of remission, while others are enacted sporadically, periodically, or in binge clusters. All are subject to triggering stimuli related to the initial experience.

Clues to the triggering stimuli can be found in current *feeling/physical symptom/ behavior combinations* that remain persistent and problematic in current life, and associated memory that continues to surface.

**Jack and the Beanstalk**: In G-OM, an analogy using the story of "Jack and the Beanstalk" is used to present the concept that practicing new behavior is like the sprouting seeds and stems of growth that must be fed and tended daily to compete with the thick tall winding beanstalk that has a behavioral giant at the top who has been wielding control. By learning to separate the self from the behavior and seeing it as a giant enemy force that also had a beginning and a reason for its development, participants can work more productively to produce creative ideas and action plans that have the potential to be effective.

**Collaboration** can happen with a number as small as two or a number as large as the group involved. If the clinician assumes control by dictating strategies or assigning alternative behavior actions without a collaborative exchange, the workload falls to the clinician and the participants do not have a chance to develop trust in their ability to develop their own behavioral plans. A workshop approach to behavioral development is very helpful at this stage.

**The Workshop Approach**: Working together in small groups or at tables, participants begin their behavioral planning workshop using the G-OM worksheets that follow. They are encourages to develop positive alternative behaviors that are self-enhancing and involve skills and abilities that are used in the pattern that is being replaced. When the new behavior is regularly practiced, a behavioral option is created. The old relied upon behavior can only be diminished when something takes its place. When an extreme state is triggered in current life, an alternative positive action that utilizes abilities used to enact the old behavior increases the probability of intensity reduction and successful replacement.

Natural abilities and developed skill that evolved within the old behavior pattern are also an established part of the person's ego and personality. The old behavior, despite its problems, is typically an action that the person can do very well. When participants realize that they have practiced skills that are useful to new alternative actions, the replenished ego becomes an additional motivating factor in daily practice. A person who has lost self-confidence, and who is weighed down by self-defeating thoughts and low self-esteem, cannot move forward without incentive and motivation. Motivation that may be initially inspired by the desire to change must be bolstered by that which can be accomplished. Behavioral change that is a positive reconstruction of an established pattern is more likely to succeed.

Natural traits and abilities are genetically expressed at the most crucial times, and develop because we are inclined toward actions that we can do. A child that sits down at a keyboard and discovers that he or she can pick out a melody will return to the keyboard. A child who finds this difficult and frustrating will not unless forced to practice. The incentive to act without provocation comes from within and can blossom into new areas when a collective structure provides an encouraging beginning.

## CASE EXAMPLE OF PATTERN EVOLUTION, SKILL, ABILITY AND INNOVATION

Tommy, age 4, lived in an abusive environment. His father was verbally and physically abusive to his mother, and verbally abusive to Tommy. The abuse mainly occurred on weekends when his father wasn't working. Tommy was accustomed to his father's behavior and felt helpless to stop it. He both feared his father and desired his attention. Sometimes his father gave him attention that was positive and everything seemed okay for a while.

But one day, his father came home early and ran over Tommy's tricycle left in the driveway. He came into the house in a rage and grabbed Tommy, hitting him several times and throwing him into his bedroom where he was ordered to remain for the rest of the day. At first Tommy felt terrified and powerless and desperate to escape his father's wrath. He didn't even understand what had happened and couldn't grasp this sudden vicious attack on his head, arms and legs. Tears flowed from his eyes and he felt a throbbing pain in his chest. He could hardly breathe and could only whimper as he fell onto his bed and tried to figure out what he had done. Then he heard his father attacking his mother and for the first time realized what it felt like to be beaten the way his mother had been, repeatedly. Suddenly his fear turned into anger and he desperately wanted to get out of his room.

For the first time, Tommy wanted to rebel in some way. He remembered that there was a box of matches on the kitchen stove that he had been warned never to touch. The kitchen was located down the hallway from his room and he knew that he could get there and back while his father was with his mother at the other end of the house. He disobeyed his father and opened the bedroom door, ran down the hallway into the kitchen, moved the stool placed next to the kitchen cabinet and climbed it to reach the matches. He returned the stool to its place and ran back to his room, shutting the door and shaking all over. He immediately reached into the box and scratched the match across the black strike-worn strip alongside the box as he had seen his mother do countless times. When the flame burst before his eyes he felt an internal explosion of sensation unlike anything he had previously experienced. He became mesmerized staring at the orange-red glowing hot flame and felt powerful for the first time in his life. He didn't even feel the burn at first when the flame reached his little fingers. When the pain finally hit, he threw the match down. Hearing voices, he picked up the burnt match and hid it and the box under his pillow. He knew from that moment that he would always keep them near and felt that he could hardly wait until he could light the match again. He found something that would help him from that day on and no one, not even his father, was more powerful than the flame.

Tommy's behavior pattern began with a lighted match. With each repetition, the flame continued to generate feelings of power and physical exhilaration (arousal) that helped him to combat his feelings of utter helplessness. His preoccupation with matches increased with each use. He began stealing a few matches each day from the kitchen and hoarding them in a variety of hiding places. He also started experimenting with lighting small fires, finding that the longer the flame lasted, the longer he could extend the desired feelings and sensations. His mother caught him with the matches one morning and scolded him for playing with them, taking them away from him. He simply stole more and became more adept at not being caught. He began playing with the matches outside and found a good hiding place behind his father's work shed where there was assorted debris and kindling wood. His fires were small at first and not noticed, until one day when the fire produced smoke that was seen by a neighbor.

This time, Tommy was punished for starting a fire and once again, the punishment had little effect. Instead, he planned to find better places to start his fires. With age, he gained freedom, and when he started school, his territory expanded. Over the next several years the small fires became larger fires; he became more adept at changing locations and escaping the scene of the blaze. Damage increased and was more frequent. Tommy felt a pervasive fear of being caught. Sometimes he promised himself that he would stop but the obsession overwhelmed his ability to resist repeating the behavior. During this time, the situation at home worsened and eventually his father and mother divorced. After the divorce, his behavior accelerated; his first major fire was started, causing extensive damage to a wooded area near several homes. People had to evacuate and a neighborhood search began for an arsonist suspected to be living in the neighborhood. Tommy was not a suspect because he had no record at the time. He moved his location to another area, but the fires got increasingly out of control. He learned better techniques and began using substances about this time to enhance his courage to plan, execute, and escape his scenes of destruction. He often thought about becoming a fire fighter so that he could remain on the scene of his fires without having to escape. This became a new preoccupation with Tommy as his behavior pattern evolved to a dangerous new level.

By the time Tommy was caught, he was a suspected arsonist and a volunteer fireman with a history of substance abuse that became the primary factor in his eventual arrest. His alcohol dependence resulted in a loss of control more noticeable than his arsonist behavior. It also affected his ability to perform as well and led to his capture and arrest.

**Identity:** When behavior is repeated, despite efforts to resist or stop, a self-identity is formed in relation to it. If the behavior is noticeable and results in negative or positive attention, identity is further influenced by how the behavior is labeled or judged by others. When self-esteem is diminished or enhanced by behavior that cannot be stopped, self-identity becomes intrinsically linked with the behavioral actions. Identity that relies on problematic behavior, whether positive appearing or negative, creates an identity void when the behavior cannot be enacted. This void, described by many as a feeling of emptiness, can generate mood fluctuation and pre-occupation with the behavior. This internal void adds to the obsessive nature of the patterns and is one of the reasons that vulnerability to mood-altering substance abuse and dependence is a prevalent factor when first introduced to those who feel this way. Many people suffering addiction describe their initial use of alcohol and other drugs as an effort to "fill a void" or "an empty feeling within."

G-OM Behavioral Exercises: The following exercise worksheets were developed to transition the information participants gained from OGP and its tools and worksheets into a beginning phase of positive-alternative behavioral development. At this phase of G-OM, other cognitive behavioral and therapy approaches compatible with this approach can be applied along with G-OM's continued therapeutic process and 12-Step support group work. The information gained in G-OM is crucial to understanding the core elements of conditions that can be resistant to treatment and present roadblocks to recovery.

## Worksheet: G-OM ALTERNATE BEHAVIOR EXERCISE

Name _____    Date _____

At present, during a 24–hour period of time, in a typical day, which of the following "feelings" seem to occur to you the *most* often? *CIRCLE* or write the feeling that is the *most* difficult for you to handle.

| | What *physical symptoms* are associated with or accompany this feeling? |
|---|---|
| Anger | |
| Bitterness | _____ |
| Boredom | _____ |
| Fear | _____ |
| Frustration | _____ |
| Hurt | _____ |
| Resentment | |
| Sadness | |
| Shame | |
| Loneliness | |
| Other: _____ | |

Approximately what percentage, or how much of the time, in a typical day, do you feel the feeling and symptoms you have named?

Less than 25% of the time: ___%   25%   50%   75%   100%

> **Note:** Human behavior engages thinking (internal) action and physical (external) action. When building a new behavior it is necessary *to actively engage and incorporate thoughts and actions — into the desired new response.*

List what you have actually done (thoughts + actions + behavior) to *relieve, reduce or stop* the feeling and symptoms you have identified – *that you have come to recognize as being a problem in your life.*_____

_____

_____

_____

Thoughts/beliefs that reduce/stop the feelings and physical symptoms, but *make the situation worse:*

_____

_____

_____

Statements/words that reduce/stop the feelings and physical symptoms, but *make the situation worse:*

_____

_____

_____

Acts that reduce/stop the feelings/physical symptoms, but *make the situation worse:*

_____

_____

_____

## G-OM Plan of Action

1) Review your list of behaviors. **One** behavior will be chosen for the beginning focus of this exercise. You may discuss your choice with your peers/counselor. Think in terms of priority. Which of these behaviors are in need of immediate attention? While this might apply to more than one behavior, your individual choice can be guided by thinking about which of these behaviors you would most like to change.

2) Once you have made your choice, make a list of the skills and natural abilities you have that are involved in the action of this behavior. You may already be aware of some of them if you have discussed this behavior with your counselor or group.

### EXAMPLE

Behavior: Lying          Skills: Creativity, Spontaneity, Imagination

It is important to acknowledge the positive skills and abilities in even the most problematic behaviors. These skills will be utilized to develop positive behavior strategies.

List of Skills/Abilities:

_____

_____

_____

3) Discuss the skills/abilities you have listed with your group and your counselor. While acknowledging them in relation to the behavior you have chosen to address, think of the many ways these skills and abilities could be used toward a positive alternative to this behavior. Develop a list of ideas. Discuss your ideas and then make a choice. Remember that you can always incorporate your other ideas along the way, and continue to develop your list.

**EXAMPLE**
Behavior: Lying                    Alternative: A creative and imaginative approach to honesty.

List of ideas:

_____

_____

_____

_____

_____

4) Now that you are about to begin your exercise, it is important to note that the behavior you have chosen to address presents risk to your recovery and the new positive alternative behavior you have chosen from your list of ideas will be addressed as if both are a **reality.** In other words, the old behavior is **not gone,** and the new positive behavior is **now an option.** It may be some time before the new behavior will completely overtake the old behavior.

Two factors are important to this process:
1. The new behavior will require daily practice in order to compete with the already existing pattern.
2. The already existing pattern of behavior may continue to be triggered until the new behavior takes hold.

The purpose of this exercise is to interrupt the dynamic *between* the **feelings and physical symptoms** when triggered, and the old behavior in order to create a "window of opportunity" for the **positive new behavior to be enacted in its place. This can only be done with practice.**

Gerwe Orchestration Method

ALTERNATIVE BEHAVIOR WORKSHEET

SUMMARY

FEELING AND BEHAVIOR COMBINATION

Name_____ Date_____

Old Combination of Feeling ⇨ Behavior

_____
_____
_____
_____
_____
_____

Feeling(s) + Physical Symptoms ⇨ Old Behavior




*New* Combination of Feeling ⇨ Behavior: Identify changes in each section below.

_____
_____
_____
_____
_____
_____

Feeling(s) + Physical Symptoms + Thoughts [*Interruption*] ⇨ Goal Behavior

Gerwe Orchestration Method

HOMEWORK:

ONE–HOUR DAILY ALTERNATIVE BEHAVIOR EXERCISE

Name_____ Date_____

Separate the hour into four 15–minute segments.

Make a commitment to daily practice at a specific time each day.
(Find a quiet place if possible.)

Investigation Segment: First 15 Minutes
Write Feelings and Physical Symptoms that trigger the unwanted behavior:

_____

_____

_____

_____

(a) Acknowledge the feelings/symptoms as a reality.
(b) Accept the reality that the feelings/symptoms you have listed have been repeatedly present in your life and will most likely reoccur.
(c) How often does the feelings/physical symptom combination occur?

_____

(d) How long can you endure these feeling/symptoms before you enact the behavior you are trying to change? _____

_____

(e) Are they sometimes more powerful than at other times? _____
Why?

_____

_____

_____

Understand that this is the first phase of "acting out" the behavior, even though at this time no action has been taken. This is the phase at which time it is important to "pull back" from the situation and begin using the second 15 minutes of this page as an interruption exercise.

## Interruption Segment: Second 15 Minutes

Practice one of the three "Interruption Techniques" options for 15 minutes:

(a) Prayer – for help, support and guidance in your commitment to positive change.

(b) Meditation – use a relaxation/breathing exercise to get into a meditative state. This prepares you for the exercise both physically and psychologically.

(c) Visualization – visualize yourself as you would like to behave. Use a role model, if helpful.

Practice daily.

## Alternative Action Segment: Third 15 Minutes

Write your ideas for a new behavior in response to the feelings you listed:

_____

_____

_____

_____

_____

(a) Choose an alternative behavior. You may eventually try several before you find the one that works best for you.

_____

_____

_____

_____

_____

(b) Practice your alternative behavior on a daily basis, at first by yourself in front of a mirror. Visualize yourself dealing effectively with a minor incident that would provoke you. Then practice with small or minor incidents which might normally provoke you. You are not ready for major incidents at this time. You will probably "act out" the old way with major episodes for some time. Remember, behavioral change takes time, and you have the rest of your life to continue your process of change. It is your *commitment to daily practice* that will take you successfully from minor to major incidents using your new positive behavior.

(c) Think about the benefits of your new positive alternative behavior. Be creative. The number of new positive alternatives is unlimited. Remember, your old behavior was repetitively practiced. It took years to become a habit. It will take you a while to learn a new behavior to take its place.

_____

_____

_____

_____

Reflection and Reward Segment: Fourth 15 Minutes

(a) Write your method of rewarding yourself: This is your reward time. Try to feel good about what you have just accomplished – an effort and beginning of positive change.

_____

_____

_____

_____

_____

(b) Keep a notebook to record your efforts.

(c) Give yourself a checkmark, a star, or some other kind of symbol every time you complete your exercise.

(d) Tell a supportive friend/sponsor/counselor. Share your success and receive positive feedback.

You are planting the seeds of new behavior that supports recovery and positive change.

# CHAPTER 6. COMPOSING STRATEGIES & CREATING SOLUTIONS

## STEP 6: WORKSHOPS, G-OM GROUP COMPOSITIONS, AND INDIVIDUAL SESSION QUESTIONNAIRE

> "What passion of hatred can it be which leads a man to lurk in such a place at such a time? And what deep and earnest purpose can he have which calls for such a trial? There, in that hut upon the moor, seems to lie the very centre of that problem which has vexed me so sorely. I swear that another day shall not have passed before I have done all that man can do to reach the heart of the mystery."
>
> — Arthur Conan Doyle. Dr. Watson in, The Hound of the Baskervilles, in The Strand Magazine

This section begins with a **Five-Question Group Composition** and concludes with the **G-OM Individual Session Questionnaire**. Every process in G-OM is inter-related and yet designed for a unique purpose. The consistency of the underlying theoretical concept enables participants to easily learn each tool, worksheet, and group process as they become more instrumental in their recovery process.

The **G-OM 5-Question Group Composition** represents the identifiable components that are formulated during pivotal experiences that continue to impact current life. The questions are designed to:

- help participants identify their most intense feeling and physical states that regularly impact daily mood-fluctuation and behavior,

- determine the approximate amount of time these states are triggered and interfere with positive life-functioning,
- determine the approximate origin of the feeling/physical symptom combinations to better understand the life span of these conditions,
- identify experiences associated with the identified states to better understand and find clues to current triggers associated with these experiences,
- identify behavior that originated during the identified experiences and determine if the behavior continues to be repeated in current life, creating problems and obstacles to recovery and rehabilitation.

The 5-Question Group Process is a group dynamic that includes a worksheet and written responses rather than verbal responses, provoking a thoughtful process that encourages self-investigation within the comforting embrace of group support. The written response approach alleviates individual concerns about sharing the identified experiences, while at the same time providing a context in which to do so. In this way, the experiences are transposed from within each person onto a worksheet for further processing.

The 5-Question Group Process teaches participants an objective and segmented approach to addressing the complexities of emotions, memory, and behavior in order to address each area with the most effective and appropriate therapeutic, medical and behavioral treatment strategies.

G-OM 5-QUESTION GROUP COMPOSITION

(Facilitate with Group Recorder Worksheet)

Participants will need a pen and a notebook surface to support the Group Recorder Worksheet, which will be filled in as the group progresses. The group facilitator begins with the first question and allows participants time to write in their responses on their worksheet. Follow this procedure with each question:

1. During the present time, in a typical 24-hour period, what is the worst, most upsetting feeling or feelings that you experience; feeling/s that can ruin your day and/or night?

   (If you identified a feeling or feelings, write them inside the *feeling response* section of the worksheet circle.)

2. When you experience the feeling/s you identified, where does this affect you in your body; what are the physical symptoms that you experience?

   (If you identified one or more physical symptoms, write them inside the *physical response section* of the worksheet circle).

3. During the present time, in a typical 24-hour period, how much of the time do you experience the feeling/s and physical symptoms you identified?

   Approximately   10%   25%   50%   75%   85%   95%

(Write the approximate percentage of time you experience the feeling/physical symptoms at the bottom of the *feeling/physical section* of the worksheet circle).

4. Do you remember the first time you experienced the feeling/s and physical symptoms you identified?

(If you were able to recall a time or an experience, write the time or something about the experience within the *vivid center section* of the worksheet circle).

5. Part One: If you recalled a time or experience when you first felt the feeling/ symptoms, describe what you did behaviorally. What did you do?

(If you identified a behavior or behaviors, write them within the *behavioral response section* of the worksheet circle).

   Part Two: If you identified a behavior or behaviors, are you still doing the behavior in a more advanced way?

   (If you identified the behavior as still present in your current life, write about it on the lines provided at the bottom of the worksheet circle).

--------

When the worksheets are completed, volunteers can share what they've identified in the remaining time available. Worksheets are collected and copies are made for each participant so that Facilitators can review them and participants still have them for continued work. Issues identified can be further processed with counselor or in other process groups.

Gerwe Orchestration Method

## GROUP RECORDER (MED) WORKSHEET

Name _____ Today's date: _____

Age: ___ Birth Year: _____

Frequency of Vivid Memory: _____

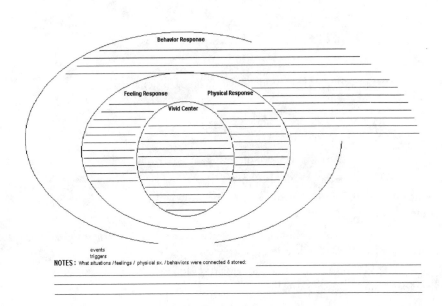

NOTES: What situations / feelings / physical sx. / behaviors were connected & stored: _____

## WORKSHEET EXAMPLE

GERWE ORCHESTRATION METHOD

# GROUP RECORDER WORKSHEET: VIVID MEMORY DYNAMIC

GROUP RECORDER WORKSHEET: VIVID MEMORY DYNAMIC

Page 1

Name ___Coby___

Today's date: __1-26-05__

Age when experience occurred: __7__   Birth Year: __1980__

Frequency of Vivid Memory: __5-6 year__

**Behavior Response**

**Feeling Response**

**Physical Response**

**Vivid Center**

WHICH WAS UNSAFE — FIRE OR WHIPPING?

→ WHEN SCARED & UPSET, PUNISH WHO-EVER SCARES/ UPSETS YOU.

HIDING = DOING DRUGS — OR ANYTHING ILLEGAL (SELLING)

FROM THE POLICE

SINCE FIRE ONLY BURNED THE ALCOHOL & NOT THE SKIN → THESE WAS NO NEGATIVE CONSEQUENCE DIRECTLY FROM THE FIRE. ONLY PUNISHMENT FROM GRANDPA → GETTING OUT OF CONTROL & CAUGHT.

SCREECH/CONFLICT SHOULD FROM FIRE CREATES ADRENALIN RUSH →

**NOTES:** What situations /feelings / physical sx. / behaviors were connected & stored? events / triggers

HIDING IN THE BACK ROOM + DOING FIRE + ALCOHOL

→ Then Married — Lost Wife & Whippings were a Blessing?

Resisted → Saved →

Isolated burst FROM → while played w/ Fire & Alcohol? + or don't LOSE CONTROL & GET CAUGHT?

Getaway → Repairing Anger   Don't Play with Fire & Alcohol? → other →

## G-OM SMALL GROUP COMPOSITIONS

The DPS works successfully for facilitating a small group process focused on behavioral development. The **Daily Prediction Scale Group Composition** has each participant share one of their worksheets and discuss setback or progress with behavioral reactions to daily life events. The group process typically takes an hour or adjusted to group population size.

The **Behavioral Action Planning (BAP)** worksheets can also be transposed into a small group composition with discussion centering on behavioral development strategies. While the DPS group process is more reflective, the BAP is facilitated as a pro-active brainstorming session.

The G-OM Individual Session Questionnaire: The Orchestration Group Process (OGP) was developed to facilitate an investigative approach to group counseling. It should be noted, however, that OGP was created from information gathered from hundreds of individual sessions, and the investigative approach that was developed within those sessions. The transposition from individual sessions into OGP sessions expanded the concept and brought about many positive outcomes. However, there still remained a need for individual sessions based on this premise for certain cases, circumstances, situations, and for therapists who prefer this approach. The G-OM Individual Session Questionnaire, beginning on the next page, is based on five major objectives:

• To identify and address the most disruptive current feeling states of the individual.

• To identify and address the physical symptoms that occur when the feeling/s are generated.

• To approximately calculate and document how often, or what percentage of time, the person experiences the identified feeling/physical symptom combination, and to what degree of intensity.

• To investigate and track the approximate origin of the identified feeling/physical symptom state, its frequency, and its progression.

• To identify and address the behavior/s constructed in response to the identified experience and track its path of problematic development to determine present and future risk factors.

G-OM INDIVIDUAL SESSION QUESTIONNAIRE #1

1. In your present life, during a typical 24-hour day or during the span of a week, can you identify the worst feeling or feelings that you typically experience? This would be the feeling or feelings that upset you the most: feelings that can transform your day or your mood.

_____

_____

_____

2. When you experience the feeling or feelings you identified, how does your body respond? Where do you feel the feeling or feelings physically in your body? Can you locate specific physical areas that are affected? Can you describe this physical response?

_____

_____

_____

3. Within a 24-hour period, or within a week, how often do you experience the feeling/ physical symptom combination you identified? What percentage of time do you feel this way?

During a 24-hour period: 10%\_\_\_ 25%\_\_\_ 50%\_\_\_ 75% \_\_\_ 100%\_\_\_\_

What percentage of a week: 10%\_\_ 25%\_\_\_\_ 50%\_\_\_\_ 75%\_\_\_\_ 100%

4. Do you remember the first time you felt this feeling/physical symptom combination? If so, describe what occurred.

_____

_____

_____

5. Do you recall what you did in response to what occurred? What behavior or behaviors did you enact?

_____

_____

_____

6. Is this feeling/physical symptom/behavior combination still present in your present life? If so, in what way, and does it create problems in your

life today?

_____

_____

_____

7. Have you ever enacted the behavior or behaviors you identified to an obsessive degree?

_____

_____

_____

8. Have you ever attempted to stop or change the behavior or behaviors you
identified?

_____

_____

_____

G-OM INDIVIDUAL SESSION QUESTIONNAIRE #2

1. In your present life, during a typical 24-hour day or during the span of a week, can you identify the best feeling or feelings that you typically experience? This would be the feeling or feelings you enjoy the most: feelings that can transform your day or your mood.

_____

_____

_____

2. When you experience the feeling or feelings you identified, how does your body respond? Where do you feel the feeling or feelings physically in your body? Can you locate specific physical areas that are affected? Can you describe this physical response?

_____

_____

_____

3. Within a 24-hour period, or within a week, how often do you experience the feeling/ physical symptom combination you identified? What percentage of time do you feel this way?
   During a 24-hour period: 10%___ 25%___ 50%___ 75% ___ 100%____
   What percentage of a week: 10%___ 25%____ 50%____ 75%____ 100%

4. Do you remember the first time you felt this feeling/physical symptom combination? If so, describe what occurred.

_____

_____

_____

5. Do you recall what you did in response to what occurred? What behavior or behaviors did you enact?

_____

_____

_____

6. Is this feeling/physical symptom/behavior combination still present in your present life? If so, in what way, and does it create problems in your life today?

_____

_____

_____

7. Have you ever enacted the behavior or behaviors you identified to an obsessive degree?

_____

_____

_____

8. Have you ever attempted to stop or change the behavior or behaviors you identified?

_____

_____

_____

# CHAPTER 7. CONDUCTING A PLAN AND EVALUATING RISK

STEP 7: THE AFTERCARE PLANNING SESSION: RISK EVALUATION AND ASSESSMENT

> "Come Watson! As to you, sir, I trust that a bright future awaits you in Rhodesia. For once you have fallen low. Let us see, in the future, how high you can rise."
>
> — Arthur Conan Doyle. Sherlock Holmes in "The Adventure of the Three Students," *The Adventures of Sherlock Holmes*

*G-Om Aftercare Planning Checklist*

**Initial Assessment**

1. Client completed the Treatment Program Admission Process including:
   - Psychosocial History
   - Clinical/Medical/Psychological Evaluation
   - Admission to G-OM 8-Week Intensive Outpatient Program
   - G-OM Assessment of Behavioral Health

2. Client completed G-OM:
   - Initial Assessment: Identification of feeling/physical symptom/behavior dynamics that are problematic and worth further exploration as treatment issues.

- Results were summarized along the six dimensions of ASAM Placement Criteria that justify treatment options.

## G-OM Concepts

3. Client has gained understanding of the nature of pivotal/novel experience in relation to:
- Persistent patterns of problematic behavior originating before addiction onset
  - Why they emerge in accessible memory
  - How the brain stores information
- The feeling/physical symptom/perceptual components of pivotal experience
  - Linking feeling/physiological dynamics with behavior construction
  - The "Art" of facilitated self-investigation
  - The use and internalization of illustrated G-OM structural concepts

## G-OM Self-Report Tools and Worksheets

4. Client has gained ability to use and understand:
- Lifespan Chart: Identifies developmental milestones and specific experiences that are uniquely significant to emotional and behavioral development.
- Daily Prediction Scale: Measures daily intensity/stress/excitement levels, identifies key extreme state triggers, identifies current feeling/physical symptom/behavior components, and risk factors.
- Memory Episode Dynamic: Addresses current accessible memories that surface and provides a method of dissemination that increases objectivity and reduces the emotional impact of the recalled experience.
- G-OM Behavioral Action Planning Worksheets: Addresses identified problematic patterns of behavior, their driving elements, and facilitates positive alternative behavioral development.

## G-OM Orchestration Group Process Participation

5. Client has participated in Orchestration Group Therapy and has gained the ability to:
- Process the dynamics of lifespan experiences in a structured group setting
  - Reframe perceptions of past experience and current events
  - Identify trigger events and stimuli
  - Identify feelings & associated physical symptoms
  - Identify behaviors that present addiction risk factors

- Ability to self-monitor on a daily basis
- Engage investigative curiosity
- Increase self-insight
- Differentiate feelings/physical symptom/ perceptual reactions and behavior response.
- Interrupt and separate emotional/perceptual (feeling + physical dynamic) from impulse to act out behavioral dynamic
- Utilize the Memory Episode Dynamic to address current and past experiences
- Utilize G-OM concepts, tools, worksheets outside of the group setting.

Workshop Group Process

6. Client has gained ability to collectively and collaboratively utilize G-OM Worksheets that help to:

- Identify natural inclinations, skills, and abilities while addressing problematic patterns of behavior
- Encourage the practices of meditation & self-monitoring skills
- Encourage creation and practice of daily positive alternative behaviors
- Develop creative coping and problem-solving skills
- Build healthy behavior patterns in response to emotional state triggers
- Fortify confidence and increase self-esteem with positive action
- Demonstrate motivation & commitment to positive alternative behavior development.

### Individual Session

7. If included, client experienced a process that helped client to:

- Process experiences that might otherwise not be addressed
- Gain insight regarding experience and its impact on current life and recovery
- Utilize the structural concept of the Orchestration Method independent of the group setting to process current states and behavior
- Implement the MED as a documented account of the session

8. Outcome Evaluation

9. Client completed G-OM Exit Interview Questionnaire that:

- Solicits anonymous feedback from clients leaving primary treatment reflecting specific relapse prevention skills learned as a result of G-OM training.

### Aftercare

10. Client collaborated with counselor to design an aftercare plan tailored

to recognize strengths and treatment accomplishments, and address risk patterns evaluated on the G-OM-PTRS (see following page) with the appropriate therapeutic and support network referral.

Note: G-OM can be utilized as a stand-alone aftercare method, or components of G-OM can reinforce co-existing aftercare programs and facilitates referral to:

- Appropriate support groups (see Behavioral Development and The Twelve Steps section)
- Further medical/psychiatric intervention referral if needed
- Continued therapy with appropriate therapist/therapeutic interventions and processes if needed
- Referral should directly relate to identified problems and risk factors, and foster positive behavioral development.

HIGH RISK IDENTIFICATION & EVALUATION: THE POTENTIAL TOWARD RELAPSE SCALE (PTRS)

Now that the client has completed the individual aftercare session, a careful and thoughtful analysis should follow. The Potential Toward Relapse Scale (PTRS) instrument is a valuable tool that can influence a re-evaluation of the initial diagnosis and facilitate appropriate aftercare planning that addresses behavior patterns that pose potential risk for relapse. The PTRS is designed to assess risk on a scale of determinants that identify behavior patterns that present risk to health and recovery. The scale also identifies strengths and positive behavior that should be recognized and acknowledged. Recognizing positive behavior is as essential to this evaluation as recognizing the risk patterns. Positive behavior and strengths are the balancing factors that can be built upon to enhance motivation. The aftercare plan should reflect each side of the behavioral spectrum. The completed behavioral exercise worksheets provide a framework that demonstrates that positive skills, abilities, and strengths can be gleaned from negative patterns and transposed into new positive alternative behavior. These existing positive elements, when recognized, can shift the balance of power from negative potential to positive measurable outcomes. The benefits of the PTRS are:

- It is an evaluation tool that can be utilized in collaboration with the client.
- It helps the client use a simple concept of scales and balances to reframe ideas about behavior and put them into a more objective perspective.
- It helps the client understand balance in relation to the underlying dynamics of behavior, and why imbalance can undermine recovery efforts.

- It helps the client continue to conceptually separate behavior from self-identity and instead view it as an entity that can be overcome with shifting balances.

- It provides a measurement of self-efficacy that helps motivate the client, while also addressing the reality of risk that must be considered for aftercare planning and referral.

## CHRONIC RELAPSE SCREENING INSTRUMENT

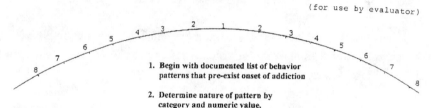

**CHRONIC RELAPSE SCREENING INSTRUMENT**

**POTENTIAL TOWARD RELAPSE SCALE** (PTRS)

(for use by evaluator)

1. Begin with documented list of behavior patterns that pre-exist onset of addiction

2. Determine nature of pattern by category and numeric value.

3. Mark total number of LOW risk patterns on left of above arc/ HIGH risk on right.

| LOW RISK | HIGH RISK |
|---|---|
| 1. patterns that indicate self-value | 1. patterns that indicate self-sabotage |
| 2. patterns that indicate acceptance of self and others | 2. patterns that indicate self-abuse |
| 3. patterns that indicate spiritual beliefs | 3. patterns that indicate life risk |
| 4. patterns that indicate self investment | 4. patterns that indicate violent aggression |
| 5. patterns that indicate positive alternative behavioral development | 5. patterns that indicate revenge/ retaliation |
| 6. patterns that indicate positive perception of family and/or environment | 6. patterns that indicate rebellion |
| 7. Patterns that indicate potential for group and support system development | 7. patterns that indicate ritual |
| 8. patterns that indicate positive interests | 8. patterns that indicate withdrawal and isolation |

(c) 1995 C.F. Gerwe    157

Each pattern has a numeric value of (1).

115

## A HIGH-RISK CASE EXAMPLE: RYAN: A RISK NOT IDENTIFIED

Ryan was admitted to addiction treatment for the third time, diagnosed as alcohol and other drug dependent. Age 20, white, male, attractive in appearance, well dressed and well groomed, personable and well mannered, Ryan was from a comfortably middle-class home and environment. Prior to admission, he had been preparing to enter a university instead of an addiction treatment center.

Chemical dependency was not his only problem. He had just violated his probation and was facing additional legal charges upon discharge from treatment. Since age 13, Ryan had accumulated a lengthy legal history, much of it not accessible due to juvenile status. His parents had provided much of this information on the family intake form, primarily out of desperation. They had previously kept Ryan's juvenile record a family secret. Ryan's insurance provider would not approve payment for another stay in addiction treatment. His parents had secured a loan. This time they expected Ryan to succeed! His father was adamant on this point.

Ryan's latest legal charge was for assault, with intent to commit bodily harm. The charge resulted in violation of probation stemming from previous assault charges. Most of Ryan's juvenile charges were related to loss of control, resulting in episodes of violence. Much of his behavior had been documented as alcohol or other drug related according to intake assessment information. Ryan's willingness to previously enter treatment had influenced the court to grant a lengthy probation instead of time served in a correction facility. This time, probation was unlikely.

There is a distinct difference in a patient entering treatment for the first time and one who has been in treatment several times, such as Ryan, particularly in relation to defenses. Ryan had few defenses left and projected an attitude and manner of cooperation and complacency. He could have easily, once again, cooperated his way through another treatment experience while presenting himself as a fairly stable, well-intentioned young man who had finally "surrendered to the program." However, this time Ryan indicated a desire to gain understanding about his behavior, which he admitted had been increasingly dangerous. His episodes of violent "acting out" had escalated. His parents related two episodes in which they had felt threatened. His former girlfriend's father had threatened to sue his parents over an incident in which he had suspected Ryan of physically abusing his daughter, although she denied it. He did file charges based on his suspicions but they were dropped due to lack of evidence. However, the charges resulted in a police arrest report.

Ryan was aware that the evidence was mounting up. He expressed an intense fear of incarceration. He had successfully hidden his pattern of violent aggression during his previous treatments. This time there was too much external evidence coupled with his growing concern for himself. After his initial stabilization phase and orientation, he entered the G-OM program. He began participation in the Orchestration Group Process by stating "I don't know why I keep losing it. Sometimes, I think, the drugs help me...they calm me. They did from the first." This was the first indication that his aggression pattern pre-existed his drug use. During his participation in OGP, he consistently identified feelings, physical symptoms and behavior associated with his escalating pattern of violence. Ryan also participated fully in the over-all addiction treatment program in which G-OM was an integral part. As he began to gain an objective understanding about his feelings, symptoms, and behavior, he also tracked a history of volatile behavior dating back to his elementary school years. Two weeks into the process, he requested an individual session to discuss an experience that he had marked as significant on his Lifespan Chart. During the individual session, Ryan shared the following experience that happened to him when he was age five: Ryan described the back yard of the large two-story house where he lived with his mother, father and older sister. The yard was surrounded by a large wooden fence with spaces wide enough to slip through. The street where they lived was lined with similar large homes, most with front porches and large back yards. Ryan described the back yard in detail. He and his sister, age six, were confined to this area during their playtime.

One day, while his sister was temporarily called inside, an older girl who lived next door, and another girl with whom she was playing, called Ryan to the fence. He said he remembered feeling safe, trusting, and eager to play with someone besides his sister. She had always watched over and protected him, but this day he felt adventurous. He recalled feeling a bit independent by taking this chance, and also felt tempted by the sight of a small blue swimming pool that he could see through the fence beyond the girls. The water in the swimming pool was shimmering in the sunlight.

The tallest girl of the two asked him if he would like to play a cop and robber game. When he agreed, she said that she and her friend would be the cops and he could be the robber, since he was a boy. Recalling that he felt anxious to please them, he slipped through the fence. They immediately pretended to arrest him and put a blindfold on him tightly covering his eyes. Then they pulled his hands behind his back, handcuffed him, and began to push him forward. He tried to resist and free his hands. He didn't like the game and wanted to go back home. Suddenly, without warning, he felt a powerful push on his back and the feeling of being thrust forward. His feet and ankles met with a soft cushiony obstacle, which propelled his upper body forward as he felt himself falling. Landing heavily on his knees, then face first downward, he felt the water splash as his face plunged into the water. Ryan described the terror that gripped his entire being as he desperately tried to breathe. While trying frantically to gain leverage with his knees and forehead, the panic increased. The more he struggled the more he slipped, until after what seemed an eternity, he lost consciousness.

After that moment, he only has vague memories of days of recovery in his bedroom. He learned that his sister, upon returning to the yard and finding him missing, heard the splashing and raced to his aid, pulling him from the water. The local rescue squad was called and arrived in time to save him. After a brief stay in the hospital, he was confined to bed for an extended period of rest.

The two girls responsible for pushing him into the swimming pool were questioned about the incident. They insisted that he had accidentally tripped and fallen while they were playing a game. His father reprimanded him for leaving the yard. His sister tried to defend him, stating that she did not believe the girls because they were doing nothing to help him when she arrived on the scene. The subject was dropped due to lack of evidence and Ryan remained silent. He said he remembers lying on his bed, staring through the bedroom window at the trees beyond, feeling tricked, hurt and ashamed, but most of all angry and determined never to be tricked again. He recalled vividly his desire to get back at them, "some way, somehow."

Ryan's silence in response to his father's criticism began a pattern that continued to evolve. His obsessive need to control situations began that day in the swimming pool. This pivotal experience changed Ryan's view of his world. From that day forward, he said he no longer trusted people or situations he could not control. His anger was not limited to the girls next door, but also to his father. Thus began an adversarial relationship between him and his father that would, on occasion, erupt into episodes of violence and abuse. As Ryan became more resistant to his father's control, his father became more determined to control him. By the time Ryan entered first grade that fall, his behavior had changed dramatically.

Ryan stated that he found the new school environment threatening because there was so much more to worry about. He did his best to make a good impression on the teacher because he viewed her as his only source of protection in the classroom; a situation he felt was impossible to control alone. His parents were strict about manners and this was something he exemplified when interacting with adults. He was the complete opposite with his peers. If someone laughed, he was sure they were laughing at him. He refused to play games that required any level of trust because of his fear of being "set up." He became increasingly hyper-vigilant and his temper was easily triggered.

The teacher, who had been observing these outbursts, contacted his parents with her concerns. Ryan remembered the day his parents came to the school. After they had the meeting with his teacher, they took him to the car for the drive home. He said he didn't know what was going on, "I knew my father was really angry. He would not talk and his face looked tight. The next thing I remember is being in my bedroom and the fear I felt while sitting on the side of my bed waiting for his punishment. Even after that day, he always made me wait for hours for my punishment." Ryan described the feelings he experienced during the time he spent waiting for "the sound of his father's footsteps and the clinking sound of his belt buckle." He described sitting silently and planning for the day he would be strong enough to over-power his father and anyone else who would try to hurt him.

Fantasizing became a daily ritual. He said it helped him deal with elementary school. He learned to control his outbursts until after school, and away from school where he could not be observed by teachers or other adults who might "inform on him." This way, he could safely deny responsibility for his actions, just like the girls who had pushed him into the pool had denied responsibility for their actions. They just lied and everyone, but his sister, believed them.

Incredibly, five years later, when Ryan was nine years old, the girl next door was attacked and raped in a nearby park. Ryan remembered overhearing his parents discuss the incident, which had shocked and outraged the neighborhood. Ryan recalled feeling excited, happy, and an overwhelming sense of satisfaction. He said, "I don't recall ever feeling that good, before or since."

After school, his growing reputation for fighting helped to reinforce his feelings of control and security when he was at school because his peers were intimidated by his behavior. He continued to try to project a positive image to his teachers but some were not so easily fooled. Once again, his behavior was reported to his parents by a concerned teacher who heard he had been fighting. His father's determination to "beat this out of him" perpetuated the power struggle between them. Ryan said their relationship improved somewhat when he entered high school because, "I discovered alcohol and got involved with some new friends that I hung out with after school. So I wasn't home as much."

Things went okay, he stated, until his first arrest. By this time, his alcohol consumption had increased substantially. He reported a daily habit that included at least one pint of bourbon and/or several cans of beer. He also began experimenting with marijuana and cocaine. With increased use of substances, his temper was once again becoming difficult to control. He reacted to any perceived act of aggression, verbal or physical, by attacking the person with fists and punches until pummeling him to the floor where he would continue until his friends or others pulled him away. He was also engaging in a violent pattern of sex with two girls. One of them told a friend that she feared Ryan. The friend reported this to the school counselor. The counselor did not follow through with any action because the girl who feared Ryan denied what she had said. The counselor, however, remained suspicious of Ryan and was eventually to be instrumental in his first admission to treatment.

When Ryan entered treatment for the first time, he did so to placate his parents and the court. He had been charged with *Assault with intent to commit bodily harm*, after seriously injuring an acquaintance after an altercation at a sporting event. This was his first adult charge. There had been many before it. There would be many to follow.

Ryan stated that his second addiction treatment attempt was in earnest, he became actively involved in the 12-Step Program, attending regular meetings and out-patient continuing-care after discharge from treatment. He reports some initial success, but stated, "I wasn't comfortable at the meetings. I didn't trust the confidentiality thing. I did get a sponsor, but that was a joke because I didn't tell him the real stuff, and I didn't want to hear him criticize me." He described his feelings of irritation and agitation in reaction to anyone who tried to guide him through the program. He said he could take it while in treatment, but not from the people at those meetings and several of them irritated him. He remained clean and sober, but his disposition and attitude deteriorated. He stated, "I just felt angry all the time and I didn't know why." He said he began to engage in sexual activity almost nightly, stating "I was even beginning to scare myself. I continued to go to meetings, but I started drinking too. It's hard to talk about this but it's getting worse. Nobody can know how much worse this is getting. It would freak you if I told you everything. But I will tell you this: Sometimes I just want to kill someone, and it doesn't matter who. The sex helps. It helps when I tie them up, I mean they let me but they really don't know how bad it is or they wouldn't because, sometimes, I feel like, uh, I mean, I come so close to doing it."

During Ryan's first two treatment experiences, his aggressively violent behavior was addressed as addiction-related behavior. However, in his case, it pre-existed his substance abuse and dependence and persisted during abstinence. What could happen to make this treatment different? This was the first time he participated in a program designed to specifically address his pre-addiction condition while he also received addiction treatment. Once his behavior patterns and their corresponding feelings and symptoms were identified, he helped to develop an individually tailored list of positive behavior alternatives based on his identified natural skills and abilities that were to be practiced daily. He was to address his feelings in daily therapy group settings and he was to follow through with cognitive behavioral therapy as a part of outpatient continuing care.

He was also referred to a clinical psychologist who specialized in sexual aggression and anger management. His willingness to disclose the presence of a dangerous pattern that had previously not been addressed made it possible for Ryan to be referred to the appropriate therapies to continue to address his condition. His upcoming court date was also a factor. He was charged with assault, but not sexual assault. He had no pending charges in this regard and there was no existing evidence to support new charges. But his record would be held in account and a prison sentence was probable. It is to his credit that he chose to take the opportunity to address in treatment what he could have continued to deny.

Ryan did go to prison. The court was not willing to give him yet another chance and sentenced him to sixteen months in a state correctional facility. Whether he continued attending AA or NA in prison is not known. Therapy was not made available. While serving his sentence, Ryan entered a Chef's school training program made available at the prison facility. There was no indication on his identified list of natural skills and abilities that he had an inclination for culinary pursuit. Other recommendations for follow-up treatment were not implemented in the prison setting in which he was incarcerated. His sexual aggression went untreated. Ryan's case example is included here for several reasons:

- It is an example of a pivotal episode that occurred outside the home environment.
- Ryan's reaction to the episode had a significant impact on his behavior. His parents reported that prior to age five, he had seemed a happy, well-adjusted child.
- His behavior had an impact on the home environment and the home environment changed in response to Ryan's behavior.
- Ryan's relationship with his father changed as a result of his father's punishment and recrimination.
- Ryan developed several patterns of behavior from an evolving series of episodes that exacerbated his initial response to his experience in the pool.
- Ryan's patterns of behavior evolved prior to, during addiction progression, and during periods of abstinence.
- Identified patterns involved in secret: fantasizing retaliation, plotting, strategizing, etc
- Identified patterns of violence and sexual aggression were sometimes covered up or minimized by parents and girlfriends: criminal juvenile history, violent sex.

- Ryan identified patterns that appeared to be positive: polite, well-mannered, engaging, but also admitted they were used as facade, to deceive and manipulate others.

- Ryan's patterns of behavior had an adverse affect on his recovery process, particularly in his support group interactions.

- Ryan's condition was not identified during childhood, continued untreated through adolescence, escalated during young adulthood and he remains at high risk. However, he does have knowledge of his need for the treatment follow-up that he helped to plan before being taken to prison, and perhaps he will follow-through upon probation.

Ryan was evaluated on the G-OM Chronic Relapse Screening Instrument, Potential Toward Relapse Scale (PTRS) at high risk for relapse and behavioral progression. Although his case is unique in relation to his lifespan experiences, his case is not unusual in relation to chronic addiction and criminal recidivism and the underlying conditions that contribute to them. G-OM is now implemented into a criminal justice pilot program in Atlanta, Georgia that was developed to reduce the recidivism rate of offenders with a history of substance abuse. Note: Ryan is a fictional case example based on G-OM case histories that remain confidential.

# CHAPTER 8. ARRANGING COLLABORATIONS FOR SUPPORT AND SUCCESS

## STEP 8: BEHAVIORAL DEVELOPMENT AND THE 12-STEP PROGRAM

> "Should you care to add the case to your annals, my dear Watson," said Holmes that evening, "it can only be as an example of that temporary eclipse to which even the best-balanced mind may be exposed. Such slips are common to all mortals, and the greatest is he who could recognize and repair them. To this modified credit I may, make some claim." — Arthur Conan Doyle. Sherlock Holmes in "The Disappearance of Lady Frances Carfax."

Yale University School of Medicine researchers now argue that adolescent drug addiction should be considered a developmental disorder associated with the changing motivational circuitry of the adolescent brain during development that makes them highly vulnerable to the effects of alcohol and other addictive drugs (Chambers et al. 2003). The Yale study looks at the role of novel experience in relation to adolescent addiction vulnerability, onset and progression. G-OM investigates the role of novel/pivotal experience in relation to pre-adolescent conditions that influence addiction vulnerability, onset, and post-treatment relapse.

Experimentation with mood-altering substances that results in mood enhancement and a temporarily altered self-perception for a youth already afflicted with a behavioral condition that diminishes self-esteem, poses a higher than norm risk for substance abuse and dependence. When substance abuse forms a precarious relationship with an existing behavioral condition, relapse is more likely to occur during recovery attempts due to the persistence of the pre-existing pattern and the interdependent relationship between the two conditions. In some cases, initial substance use alleviates the need or desire to enact the behavior, but behavioral remission is usually temporary. The behavior tends to re-emerge as addiction progresses and loss of control increases. Another crucial time for potential re-emergence is during vulnerable periods of addiction recovery. When the behavioral condition is re-triggered during recovery and persists, mood fluctuation, low self-esteem, and additional problems can sabotage progress and promote risk for remission and relapse. G-OM asserts that pre-addiction behavioral conditions create high risk for relapse and recidivism and need to be co-currently treated at the earliest possible stages of addiction treatment.

**Pattern Development and SUDS:** It can be mistakenly assumed that the problematic behaviors are a result of substance abuse, in cases where the behavior pattern was well established prior to addiction onset. G-OM helps to determine whether or not the co-occurring behavioral disorder pre-existed or resulted from substance abuse/addiction. If the disorder originated during addiction progression, it is more likely to diminish with traditional recovery methods and the 12-Step Program. If it preceded substance abuse/addiction, a more intensified treatment approach is advisable due to the entrenched nature of the behavior pattern.

**Addictive behavior** is a term associated with behavior that originates and develops during addiction onset and progression. Addictive behaviors that develop to support or camouflage substance abuse or dependence typically diminish with prolonged abstinence and active 12-Step Program participation. Pre-addiction patterns of problematic behavior originating during pivotal experiences that occur during the developmental period are more resistant to treatment and tend to persist during addiction recovery if not effectively addressed. Pre-addiction patterns can re-emerge when the "vulnerable self" can no longer additionally rely on mood-altering substances, and when emotional dysregulation begins to intensify and interfere with daily progress. Counselors and family members are often frustrated and mystified when the person in recovery expresses sincere commitment, and begins making progress in many areas, only to sabotage this progress with behavior that is difficult to explain or understand. The recovering person enacting the sabotaging behavior can also become frustrated and begin to experience preoccupation with the behavior and thoughts of substance use.

Behavioral conditions that interfere with a new and positive relationship with life and recovery can produce an internal struggle that depletes motivation and self-regard, while creating a reverse momentum of inevitability towards relapse. Relapse studies indicate that craving and withdrawal symptoms are major factors in relapse. Another recognized significant factor is negative emotional state. Recognizing the role of pivotal experience in problematic behavioral development helps us to understand more about negative emotional states, arousal states, and the behavior that is driven by them. Understanding and treating these conditions is a necessary and proactive approach to reducing chronic addiction relapse.

G-OM is a process of facilitated self-investigation that helps the client determine if patterns of behavior are a current risk factor to addiction recovery. Gained understanding about how these patterns originate, evolve, and influence daily life helps the client to recognize conditions and associated behavior that could potentially sabotage recovery. Clients learn the importance of integrating new positive alternative strategies and actions into their support group attendance and the practice of recovery principles. The following reprint of The Twelve Steps of Alcoholics Anonymous is followed by a step-by-step brief synopsis of how positive behavioral development can coincide with the 12-Step Program.

THE TWELVE STEPS OF ALCOHOLICS ANONYMOUS

1. We admitted we were powerless over alcohol — that our lives had become unmanageable.

2. Came to believe that a Power greater than ourselves could restore us to sanity.

3. Made a decision to turn our will and our lives over to the care of God as we understood Him.

4. Made a searching and fearless moral inventory of ourselves.

5. Admitted to God, to ourselves, and to another human being the exact nature of our shortcomings.

6. Were entirely ready to have God remove all these defects of character.

7. Humbly asked Him to remove our shortcomings.

8. Made a list of all persons we had harmed, and became willing to make amends to them all.

9. Made direct amends to such people wherever possible, except when to do so would injure them or others.

10. Continued to take personal inventory and when we were wrong promptly admitted it.

11. Sought through prayer and meditation to improve our conscious contact with God as we understood Him, praying only for knowledge of His will for us and the power to carry that out.

12. Having had a spiritual awakening as the result of these steps, we tried to carry this message to alcoholics, and to practice these principles in all our affairs.

\* \* \* \*

The Twelve Steps are taken from *Alcoholics Anonymous* (Third Edition), published by A.A. World Services, Inc., New York, NY, pp. 59-60.

1. Positive-Alternative Behavioral Development and the 12 Steps

What does the concept of powerlessness have to do with the behavior you are addressing? During the beginning stages of recovery, you have been introduced to the Step One concept of admitting powerlessness over alcohol and other drugs, and that your life had become unmanageable. The concept of powerlessness can also be applied to behavior that repeats again and again despite consequences. Now that you have identified your most problematic patterns of behavior and determined those that were developed prior to your substance abuse, how does Step One help you accept the overwhelming nature of your behavioral condition, while helping you develop and practice new positive actions? Behaviors that have created problems in your life, negatively affected your self-esteem, placed your health, relationships, and life in jeopardy, and have persisted despite your efforts to change, act much like your addiction to substances. Once these behaviors are understood in how they form and develop, there is hope in the knowledge that the power they have over you now must be challenged by daily practice of new behavior, and believing in a power greater than yourself that can help you meet this challenge. How do you understand the concept of powerlessness in relation to the behaviors you've identified?

_____

_____

_____

_____

_____

2. Step Two introduces the concept of belief in a power greater than self.

How can developing believe in a power greater than self help you to address your most problematic behavior? Have you ever said to yourself or others: "I will never do that again." "I couldn't help it." "I didn't mean to say that." "Why did I do that?" "I wouldn't have done that if he or she hadn't provoked me." "I acted without thinking." "This is just me, who I am." During the process of G-OM, you've learned about how your most significant life experiences impact the way certain behaviors are formed. You've also learned that studies in recent years indicate that new learning and behavior can create new activity in the brain that can have a beneficial and restorative impact on both mental and physical health. And yet with all we have learned from scientific advancements, the concept of a power greater than self that is more powerful than our human efforts continues to help us recognize the importance of spiritual development. The process of spiritual development in relation to heath and recovery is now being widely accepted in traditional medicine. How has your behavior affected you spirituality? Is there a gap between your self-worth and your belief in your potential for spiritual growth that is directly related to your behavior? Feelings that underlie your behavior (for example, guilt, shame, anger, resentment) can also widen the chasm. Is there anything creating a gap between you and your ability to accept that you are worthy of spiritual connection?

_____

_____

_____

_____

_____

_____

3. Step Three involves the decision to turn your will and your life over to the care of God, as you understand Him.

Is your behavior standing in the way of your decision to turn your will and life over to the care of a higher power? And if you have made the decision, does it seem as though your effort was half-hearted and insincere due to continuation of your behavior? Is one or more of your identified patterns of behavior blocking your spiritual progress? If so, maybe a new behavior strategy is in order. What new alternative behavior can help you to move through this blockade? What positive action can you take? Consider the understanding and objectivity you have gained by increasing your knowledge of how patterns form and evolve, and why some are so persistent. What kind of action can be implemented into your daily activities to support and help you to sustain a commitment to spiritual development?

_____

_____

_____

_____

4. Step Four involves a searching and fearless moral inventory of self.

Writing a Fourth Step can be a difficult process for many. However, during the G-OM process, you have worked diligently on your Life-span charting assignment; this is a valuable resource for beginning Step Four. The Life-span Chart you have completed to date will provide you with a structured format from which to work. You have also gained objectivity in being able to identify the most crucial events and problematic conditions of your past and present life. Your life span chart helps you to begin the process of examining your life in perspective. By using this guideline, you can review your life in stages and determine those events/episodes, feelings, symptoms, perceptions, and behaviors that will be addressed during the Step-Four process. This in-depth review of your life will help to prepare you for Step Five, help you evaluate the progress you have made, and help you to identify the problems that continue to persist. You have gained understanding of how behavior, constructed during experiences that produced your most highly intense to extreme states, originated and developed into deeply entrenched patterns that have persisted despite your efforts to stop or change the behavior. How would you assess these patterns in relation to a moral inventory? What insights have you gained about self in relation to behavior constructed during your most pivotal experiences? What is your responsibility today in relation to these behaviors now that you know that positive alternative behavior can be developed and spiritual connection embraced?

_____

_____

_____

_____

_____

_____

5. Step Five involves an admission to God, yourself, and another human being the exact nature of your wrongs.

How has your understanding changed about yourself in relation to your behavior? Allow the objectivity you have gained to enable you to be honest and forthright in your disclosure. Determine the differences in behavior that developed prior to the onset of addiction, and behavior that developed during your addiction progression. In admitting the exact nature of your wrongs, and the resulting consequences to self and others, how has your gained understanding about the origin and nature of your most problematic behavior helped you address your disclosure more honestly? With the help of your sponsor, address the wrongs you have identified, while also recognizing the nature of the behavior associated with those wrongs, in order to gain a balanced perspective. What information can you share with your sponsor that is related to your most problematic patterns of behavior? Describe the new positive alternative actions you are practicing.

_____

_____

_____

_____

_____

_____

6. Step Six involves readiness to have God remove all defects of character.

How does your behavior influence your character? Are the feelings, physical symptoms, and thoughts you identified in relation to your most problematic states and behavior part of your character? When you think about these questions, consider how developing new patterns of behavior that generate positive feelings that grow from personal growth can develop your character in new ways. Behavior that developed during the addiction process developed to support your addiction and should diminish with abstinence and recovery. Behavior patterns that were constructed in relation to your most pivotal experiences are less likely to diminish or be easily "removed" until alternative patterns are developed to replace them. In addition, life will continue to present situations that produce intense feelings and physical symptom states that may trigger the impulse to enact the problem behaviors. How can spiritual growth and personal effort increase your ability to enact the new behavior instead, and also further develop your character? Do you believe daily practice of new behavior is necessary to have defects of character removed?

_____

_____

_____

_____

_____

_____

7. Step Seven requires that we humbly ask God to remove our shortcomings.

   Can the approach described above, following Step Six, be applied to address-ing your shortcomings, and how?

_____

_____

_____

_____

_____

_____

8. Step Eight requires that you make a list of all persons you have harmed, and become willing to make amends to them all.

   Is it possible to make amends, and then continue to enact behavior that re-quires you to make amends on a regular basis? What can you do if you find your-self repeating behavior that requires you to repeatedly make amends? G-OM has taught you to approach behavioral development as a life-long process. New alter-native strategies can be initiated at any time. Would you consider a behavior that persists despite your efforts a hopeless defeat, or will you continue to innovate and come up with better behavioral strategies to practice and replace your most persistent problematic behavior?

_____

_____

_____

_____

_____

9. Step Nine addresses the issue of not making direct amends when to do so would injure.

In a sense, this step requires you to assess situations and determine to do no harm. How would you go about making this determination? How does behavioral development increase your ability to make the right decisions about making amends? How does evidence of your positive behavioral efforts, character and spiritual development enhance your ability to make amends that might otherwise be rejected?

_____

_____

_____

_____

_____

10. Step Ten requires that you continue to take personal inventory and when you are wrong promptly admit it.

The problematic behavior you identified during the G-OM process developed over many years. Some may have originated in your early childhood. Others may have originated and developed during your pre-adolescence, adolescence or during adulthood. Some may have originated during periods of life-stage change, or in response to current life-changing events. Even with your best efforts, life will continue to present you with events and challenges that can change and shape you in many ways. A commitment to periodic re-evaluation and regular introduction of positive alternative actions can continue to revitalize your lifelong personal growth process. One new positive alternative behavior introduced into your present life sets the stage for all those that you continue to develop. Like a domino effect, one new behavior leads to another. As a result, your inventory continues to reflect what you have worked hard to achieve. Describe a new behavior that you have been practicing that can be listed in your personal inventory. Describe the effort involved in your daily practice.

_____

_____

_____

_____

_____

11. Step Eleven seeks through prayer and meditation to improve conscious contact with the God of your understanding, praying only for knowledge of His will for you and the power to carry that out.

The G-OM behavioral alternative worksheet exercises also encourage prayer and meditation to help you begin the process of daily practice of new positive alternative actions. Step Eleven inspires belief in the knowledge that you are not alone in this process and will be given the strength to proceed through the challenges that accompany change. How have you incorporated a spiritual or meditative process into your daily thoughts and practice? How has this been helpful to you in your personal process of behavioral development?

_____

_____

_____

_____

_____

12. Step Twelve addresses the spiritual awakening that results from the steps and encourages this message to be carried to alcoholics and the practice of these principles in all affairs.

During G-OM, you worked hard to investigate self, process experiences, identify problematic conditions, begin a behavioral development process, and address sabotaging factors to your recovery process. You have gained understanding about factors that create roadblocks to behavioral and spiritual development and the underlying conditions that create these roadblocks. You have progressed through a challenging process and are now prepared to continue in an aftercare environment that includes the 12-Steps. How have you come to understand how behavioral development can work in relation to the 12-Step Program?

_____

_____

_____

_____

_____

_____

# CHAPTER 9. THE FINALE: THE G-OM EXIT QUESTIONNAIRE

> "I never hear of such a case as this that I do not think of Baxter's words, and say, 'There but for the grace of God, goes Sherlock Holmes.'" — Arthur Conan Doyle. "The Boscombe Valley Mystery," *The Adventures of Sherlock Holmes.*

Now that you have completed the G-OM program, having participated in all lectures, workshops, and group processes, please place a checkmark by the answer that best represents your response to the following questions/statements:

1) As a result of my participation in this program, I have gained the ability to identify and describe feelings that present risk factors in my recovery process.
   (1) Strongly Disagree____ (2) Disagree____ (3) Agree____ (4) Strongly Agree____

2) As a result of my participation in this program, I have gained the ability to identify and describe physical symptoms that are generated by the identified feelings.
   (1) Strongly Disagree____ (2) Disagree____ (3) Agree____ (4) Strongly Agree____

3) As a result of my participation in this program, I have gained the ability to identify perceptions (thoughts) that accompany the combined feelings/symptoms states identified.
   (1) Strongly Disagree____ (2) Disagree____ (3) Agree____ (4) Strongly Agree____

4) As a result of my participation in this program, I have gained the ability to identify behavioral patterns that are associated with the combined feelings/symptoms/perceptions identified.

(1) Strongly Disagree____ (2) Disagree____ (3) Agree____ (4) Strongly Agree____

5) As a result of participation in this program, I have gained the ability to identify situations that are associated with the feelings/symptoms/perceptions/behavior combinations identified.

(1) Strongly Disagree____ (2) Disagree____ (3) Agree____ (4) Strongly Agree____

6) As a result of participation in this program, I have gained the ability to review my lifespan, up to this point in my life, with increased objectivity.

(1) Strongly Disagree____ (2) Disagree____ (3) Agree____ (4) Strongly Agree____

7) As a result of participation in this program, I have gained the ability to identify significant lifespan periods and experiences that are associated with the combinations identified.

(1) Strongly Disagree____ (2) Disagree____ (3) Agree____ (4) Strongly Agree____

8) As a result of participation in this program, I have gained better understanding of my behavior in relation to problematic patterns that pose risk to my recovery.

(1) Strongly Disagree____ (2) Disagree____ (3) Agree____ (4) Strongly Agree____

9) As a result of my participation in this program, I have learned to monitor my feelings, physical symptoms, perceptions, and behavior for risk factors within each 24-hour period.

(1) Strongly Disagree____ (2) Disagree____ (3) Agree____ (4) Strongly Agree____

10) As a result of my participation in this program, I have gained the ability to effectively self-report high-risk symptoms to my therapist, support group, and/or physician when triggered.

(1) Strongly Disagree____ (2) Disagree____ (3) Agree____ (4) Strongly Agree____

11) My ability to identify and self-report high risk symptoms and behavior improves my ability to approach my recovery more effectively.

(1) Strongly Disagree____ (2) Disagree____ (3) Agree____ (4) Strongly Agree____

12) My participation in this program has increased self-understanding to the degree that I have gained the ability to approach my recovery and behavioral development more effectively.

(1) Strongly Disagree____ (2) Disagree____ (3) Agree____ (4) Strongly Agree____